C LASSIC

The Mr.Whippy Story

S TEVE T ILLYER

N O S T A L G I A   R O A D

First published by
Transpennine Publishing 2003

This edition published by
Crécy Publishing 2013

A CIP record for this book is available from the British Library

ISBN 9 781908 347091

Printed in Malta by Melita Press

Crécy Publishing Limited
1a Ringway Trading Estate
Shadowmoss Road
Manchester M22 5LH

www.crecy.co.uk

Front Cover: Children queue at the Mr.Whippy van in this evocative picture taken *circa* 1962. The slogan states try the 'new' ice cream, although this picture was taken some three years after the launch of Mr.Whippy. Note the smart salesman in his bow tie.

Rear Cover Top: Here we see a 1970's Morison Elecrtofreeze Bedford CF restored in recent years by Rupert Grint of Harry Potter fame. The departure from the original pink & cream livery works well with the addition of a white roof. *Photo courtesy of Classic Van & Pickup magazine*

Rear Cover Bottom: This official company picture from the early 1960's clearly shows the first fully formed Mr.Whippy livery. This livery was maintained throughout the early years of Commer/Karrier production.

Contents Page: Fully restored in recent years to its original specification, this short wheelbase Electrofreeze of Southhampton built Commer/Karrier now forms part of the Whitby Heritage Collection at Crewe.

All the illustrations, unless otherwise indicated, are from the author's collection.

Contents

Acknowledgements   4

Introduction   5

The Early Years   6

Birth of a Brand   10

Tractor Vaporising Oil   15

Coach-Built Vans   16

Empire Building   24

The Forte Years   32

The Wall's-Whippy Years   38

The Brand Image   44

Mr Whippy Overseas   48

The Pied Piper   56

The Opposition   58

The Wall's Ice Cream Story   60

Index   64

Acknowledgements

PETER Hopkins; Alan Earnshaw; Ice Cream Alliance; John Adams; Mike Allen; Aztec Oils Ltd; Andy Ballisat; Joan Barras; Jennie Tillyer; Stan Buchan; Antonio Catalano; Geoff Caverhill; Denise Conklin; Kevin & Margaret Donovan; John Duke; Alan Earnshaw; Leslie Edwards; Stan Gordon; Lisa Green; Jock Gwilt; John James; Kevin Jennings; Brian Lilley; Michael Lloyd; Keith & Fred Metcalf; Howard Mitchel; Terry Newman; Brent Owen; Anthony Pacitto; Melanie Peart; Steve Pheasant; Pim Reinders; Matthew Richardson; Hilary Robertson; Karl Rozzo; Terry Shaw; Shell UK; Colin Tarr; Kathryn Taylor; Ian & Nick Smith; Bob & Robby Staff; Jim Valenti; Burt Williams; Robin Weir; Stuart Whitby; Jean Yates; Noel McCullough; Jenny Kindell.

This and many other such adverts were placed in the Ice Cream Alliance journal during the formative years of Mr.Whippy. Not only was the company trying to attract individual drivers, but also fleet operators willing to join the brand as franchised agents. *Ice Cream Alliance*

Introduction

As our title states, this book is all about 'Mr.Whippy'. Now! Many readers may be forgiven for thinking that this all about 'soft ice cream' rather than a famous brand. The Mr.Whippy brand has long become a popular term for soft ice cream. Generic terminology is obviously not a new phenomenon and, in many ways, is a form of flattery. How many of us refer to our vacuum cleaner as a 'Hoover' or a ballpoint pen as a 'Biro' or indeed a spa bath as a 'Jacuzzi'? However, our subject matter here deals with that famous brand found on those ubiquitous pink and cream vans that were much loved by the children of the 1960s and 1970s.

Following years of rationing, Britain finally broke free from post-war austerity as the 1950s came to a close. In 1959 Cliff Richard recorded his first number one hit, the ground breaking Morris Mini was launched and London Transport's ground breaking Routemaster bus joined Austin's new FX4 taxi on the streets of London — and the public were about to get ice cream 'American Style'.

Ice cream had always been a favourite of the rich and famous but its general availability to the masses through mobile sales was only really developed between the two World Wars. It was in London in the early 1920s that T. Wall & Sons launched its now famous 'Stop Me And Buy One' trikes. This proved an immediate success and by the outbreak of World War 2, thousands of 'Wallsie trikes' were a common sight up and down the country. Ice cream mobiling had arrived and the people loved it!It is, therefore, fitting that the story of 'Mr.Whippy' is well and truly woven into the fabric of Wall's ice cream, the largest and commercially most successful ice cream company in the UK to date.

The cessation of hostilities in 1945 saw the gradual re-introduction of mobile sales which slowly gathered momentum throughout those post-war austerity years. As rationing gave way to the consumer boom of a 'live now, pay later' Britain, an explosion of mobiling activity took full advantage of the newly acquired surplus income being enjoyed by a much wider section of society.

Over 60 years on from its introduction to Britain's streets, Mr.Whippy is still a name synonymous with 'soft ice cream'. So read on and enjoy a nostalgic trip down Memory Lane. Yippee! — It's Mr.Whippy!

Steve Tillyer

The Early Years

As with many ice cream stories, it will come as no surprise to find that this one has its roots in 19th century Italy. A young man called Enrico Facchino and his wife, Angela Maria, from a town called Sora just south of Rome in the province of Frosinone, decided to start a new life and chose Britain as their new home in the late 1890s.

The two settled in Birmingham, where Enrico initially carried on his trade of shoemaking. Soon the family began to expand with the arrival of Anthony followed by a further three boys and six girls. Enrico was a hard worker with ambition and, before long, he opened a shop selling general goods and imported Italian foods and wine, which he sold to the local Italian community. Things were a whole lot different in those days, as Enrico used to have to go to the docks in London and Hull to acquire his produce.

It wasn't long before he and Angela Maria started to manufacture their own ice cream, which they traded from handcarts. Subsequently a horse and cart were bought, which allowed Enrico to trade further afield, while the older children took out the handcarts. So ice cream soon became an important part of the family business. The ice cream trade in Birmingham was expanding, and Enrico saw an opportunity to offer manufacturing facilities to local Italians who wanted to produce their own ice cream products. With the hostilities of World War 1 fading, Enrico decided to open what can only be described as a 'communal' ice cream factory.

A dozen or so local Italians leased his premises and equipment in order to make their own ice cream. At this time Enrico's wife would run the shop with their eldest daughter, Mary. Times were hard, so starting work at 4am was quite normal as they had to make the ice cream before starting work in the shop. It was a slow process in those old ice-and-salt freezers, so an early start ensured that plenty of ice cream would be ready for Enrico, along with his sons and daughters, to trade. In the Birmingham area known as 'Little Italy' there were numerous ice cream traders. By this time, the use of biscuit cones and wafers had become commonplace, and as such, gave rise to

Enrico and his wife Angela Maria established the family business in Birmingham during the early part of the 20th century. Their shop in 'Little Italy' specialised in selling Italian goods and produce and then, later on, their own ice cream, which became a significant part of their business.
Peter Hopkins

Right: The Facchino biscuit factory had beautiful gardens, which were a particular source of pride and joy to its owner, Enrico Facchino. *Peter Hopkins.*

Left: This picture was taken in 1908 and it shows a Devoti's Italian ice cream cart in Birmingham. It is included in this book on Mr.Whippy because the expanding Italian ice cream businesses prompted Enrico Facchino to open a small factory in the city just after World War 1. His new factory offered the growing Italian community the opportunity to produce its own ice cream. *Peter Hopkins.*

Below: This rather poor quality photograph was taken in Birmingham in 1959, and shows one of the very first Mr.Whippy Commer vans built by MTS of Feltham. These prototype vans had the Coventry Victor TVO engined generator sets, which badly overheated. The forward-hinged side-door would later become rear-hinged to allow the door to fasten to the rear panel in the open position. *Ice Cream Alliance*

a new opportunity. Enrico, along with his eldest son Anthony, saw the possibilities of producing ice cream biscuits, cones and wafers for their friends and rivals alike.

This idea took shape in the purchase of a factory in Bradford Street, and was the start of what was arguably to become one of the largest producers of ice cream biscuits in the country. Enrico's second eldest son, Paul, became the factory engineer. He was mainly self-taught and was responsible for installing and maintaining the wafer and cone machines. He then went on to install an automated production line that radically increased productivity and reduced wastage.

Enter Dominic Facchino, Enrico's third eldest son and the man who was later to become the driving force behind the launch of Mr.Whippy. Dominic was sent out on the road, with the company's first salesman (Walter Relph), to promote and sell their products. At this time Enrico had entrusted the administration and direction of the company to Anthony. However, one suspects that, on a day-to-day basis, this was far from the truth, with Enrico still being the power behind the throne.

The company became so successful that it soon outgrew the Bradford Street factory and had to look for much larger premises. Anthony took on the main responsibility for this and eventually found a suitable site in the Ward End district of Birmingham. It was then decided that the best way forward was for the company to design and build its own factory to meet their growing needs.

From his experience at Facchino Biscuits, Meddocream and the Canadian ice cream company Neilsons, Dominic Facchino went on to establish a brand that has simply become part of our language. The young man standing eighth from right is Peter Hopkins, who can best be described as Dominic's right hand man, particularly during the formative years at Mr.Whippy. Much of this book could not have been written without Peter's superb memory and his collection of archive material. *Peter Hopkins*

Anthony, along with his brothers and, of course, Enrico, then planned the building of their new factory. The new factory, which opened in 1925, was immediately fronted by beautiful gardens — inspired by the 'governor' Enrico — and soon became a local landmark. A new limited company was formed at this time under the name of Facchino's Purity Biscuits Ltd with the four Facchino brothers as directors. Anthony became the Managing Director, Paul was the Works Director, Dominic the Sales Director and Joseph the Production Director.

Much later the company developed an ice cream powder, which, when combined with water, produced an ice cream mix. This product was marketed through a new company called Meddocream Ltd. In the 1950s national ice cream manufacturers, such as Wall's, Lyons, Eldorado and Neilsons, were perceived to be a threat to the existence of the localised manufacturers — who were often small family firms — so Dominic Facchino devised a plan known as 'The Meddocream Scheme'.

Selected local ice cream manufacturers were invited to join the scheme, which was marketed under the Meddocream trade name. The powder was packed in 28lb tins that enabled customers to manufacture 'Freshly Made Ice Cream' from their own premises. More importantly, it allowed the small producer to comply with the Ice Cream Heat Treatment Regulations that had been introduced in 1948. The powdered mix eventually gave way to a freshly manufactured mix made from raw materials to a recipe formulated by Meddocream.

In 1956, the growth of the Meddocream organisation, prompted a successful takeover bid by Neilsons, owned by the Canadian entrepreneur Garfield Weston. Dominic Facchino remained and was appointed as Managing Director of the subsidiary, but Anthony Facchino continued in the same role at the biscuit company, which was later brought under the Garfield Weston umbrella.

As a result of his experience in the family business, Dominic, in particular, had always been aware of the popularity of freshly made soft ice cream and, indeed, the Facchino biscuit company had already developed a special XL cone for soft serve ice cream. The company supplied approximately half the 730 or so Woolworth stores in the UK, and, for those are not old enough to remember, nearly all these stores sold ice cream. Some stores had two ice cream selling points, one for hard and one for soft ice cream, with the latter being produced in vertical batch freezers. In this situation, the supply of XL cones was always four to five times greater than hard ice cream cones, thus proving the popularity of soft ice cream.

Legend has it that in the late 1950s, Dominic would spend a lot of his time in ice cream queues in and around the Birmingham area, observing, listening and sampling ice cream. Whether or not this is true, he certainly knew what the public wanted, and that was freshly made soft serve ice cream. However, little did he know that within a few years, he would be dubbed by some as 'The Ice Cream King'.

Birth of a Brand

ALTHOUGH Dominic Facchino continued to work for Garfield Weston at a senior management level, he was an entrepreneur at heart, and, I'm sure, longed to be back paddling his own canoe. In 1958 he visited America. It's not known why he was there, but he certainly had meetings with the Conway Brothers, the founders of Mister Softee. The story goes that, whilst there, he saw one of the Conway brothers' ground breaking 'ice cream stands on wheels'. The impact of these 'trucks' on Dominic was such that he immediately entered into negotiations with the Conways in an effort to secure the Mister Softee franchise in the UK. This was not to be, as the Conways were obviously more impressed by the stature of Smiths of Gateshead who subsequently acquired the UK Mister Softee franchise.

Undeterred, Dominic returned home to the UK secure in the knowledge that mobile soft ice cream had immense possibilities. He quickly set about planning (with business colleagues) the best way forward. An article in the trade press explains what happened next. 'The enterprise began as a joint effort by Dominic Facchino, of the once famed biscuit family and Mr. E. Pacitto of Mylo's ice cream, well-known around West London and Southend, with the agency for the Italian Carpigiani soft ice cream freezers which were made the vital part of the roving "factory on wheels"...'

By late 1958 the Mr.Whippy concept was formulated. Dominic gave up his lucrative £5,000-a-year job with Neilsons and formed a £100 company based in Leamington Spa. Joining him on the payroll were his two sisters, Philomena and Stella, along with a trusted colleague, friend and nephew Peter Hopkins, who also gave up a well-paid job to join the embryonic Mr.Whippy team.

It was decided that the best way forward was to set up a pilot scheme of six vans in Birmingham and monitor the public's response to the 'new' ice cream factories on wheels. A similar scheme in London was soon to follow. Although confidence in the Mr.Whippy concept was high, it was nevertheless a big gamble when considering that five hard vans could be purchased for the cost of one Mr.Whippy van. This cost, as we will see later, dramatically reduced.

Dominic decided to use an advertising agency — Longleys & Hoffman of Birmingham — to help create a professional and uniquely identifiable image. Dominic worked closely with Mr L. A. Binns, from the agency, to arrive eventually at the now famous Mr.Whippy brand, although the prototype vans in the pilot scheme had a much simpler livery. They knew that the Mister Softee vans, whch were soon to be launched, would be blue and white, so pink and cream became an

All looking very smart for the this publicity shot for the brochure called 'Frozen Assets'. When this was published in late summer 1962, Mr.Whippy had become a major player in the world of ice cream mobiling. *Peter Hopkins.*

This photo of an MTS-built 'Mr.Whippy' van in Mylo's livery was probably taken at the 1961 Commercial Motor Show. Mylo's operated the Mr.Whippy pilot scheme in west London. *Peter Carverhill*

Dominic Facchino was the driving force behind the launch and subsequent success of Mr.Whippy. He retired to the Channel Islands and sadly died just before the first edition of the Mr.Whippy book was published in 2003. *Peter Hopkins*

Here we see Ernest Pacitto with one of his vans at the Commercial Motor Show. He was certainly a key player in the very early days of Mr.Whippy and is thought to be responsible for much of the vans' design at MTS coachbuilders, as well as the introduction of the Carpigiani ice cream machine to the new world of soft ice cream mobiling. *Anthony Pacitto*

obvious choice for Dominic. He wanted to create a powerful, yet uncluttered image to rival the American Mister Softee brand.

The now familiar Greensleeves chime was adopted along with a smiling faced Mr.Whippy man, which endures to this day as one of the most iconic ice cream brand trademarks. The Mr.Whippy man wore a Henry VIII style bonnet and was given 'dancing feet', the end result being an instantly identifiable brand image to rival the American Softee brand's 'Conehead' trademark.

The first vans were introduced in April 1959 and worked from the newly acquired premises in Burbury Street, in the Lozells area of Birmingham. The first van was driven by Ted Vaughan who later became a senior supervisor! A new company — Mr.Whippy Ltd — was formed on 1 April 1959 with four Facchino directors, Dominic, Paul, Joseph and Stella. A sister operation of six Mr.Whippy vans soon followed in Hounslow, West London, run by Ernest Pacitto, a business associate of Dominic's.

Pacitto already operated vans under the Mylo's brand in West London and Southend-on-Sea and he also produced the ice cream mix for the Mr.Whippy London pilot scheme. He was the UK agent for Carpigiani of Bolognia and, therefore, perfectly placed to convince Carpigiani to develop a van model of its twin-barrelled 'Doppia' freezer. This move proved to be a key element in the operational success of Mr.Whippy and also established the reputation of this Italian manufacturer as a leader in mobile soft-serve machines.

Through to the mid-1960s, Warwick House, Leamington Spa was the hub of Mr.Whippy's operations. *Peter Hopkins*

In fact, Ernest Pacitto held the Carpigiani franchise for several years until it was taken over by Morrisons of Southampton. Mobilers now take the popular Carpigiani machine for granted. However, in 1958, no soft ice cream machines were specifically designed for vans. In fact, the Sweden Freeze machines used in the early years by Mister Softee were simply shop models with the wheels removed. It is interesting to note the lack of local and national media coverage during the launch of Mr.Whippy. This apparently was a deliberate strategy, as Dominic felt that by keeping his head down, he would gain valuable time to establish Mr.Whippy before the big firms caught on.

However, some limited TV advertising was said to have been used used to good effect in Birmingham during the spring and early summer of 1959. It should be noted that Lyons was ahead of the game with its involvement in the launch of the Mister Softee brand a month earlier. Dominic's fear of the 'big boys' was surely aimed at the other big players such as Wall's, which, fortunately for Dominic, demonstrated an apparent total disinterest in soft ice cream. It's fair to say that this was quite common at the time, as many in the trade were extremely sceptical about the future of soft ice cream mobiling and said that it was just a fad, due to its high capital and maintenance costs. Mr.Whippy and Mister Softee were about to prove them all wrong!

Some of the early operators were far-sighted and continued to expand with Mr.Whippy. They proved that, despite the high capital costs involved, soft ice cream mobiling was a lucrative business and here to stay. Yet, as the problems of the post launch period became resolved, new franchisees were brought on-line for the 1960 season. Ice cream operators such as Ken Reynolds of Grays, Harry Williams of Barking, George Cooper of Welwyn Garden City, Leo Di Mascio of Mitcham and John Di Mascio of Erith were all in the vanguard of soft ice cream mobiling.

From the outset, the rapid growth of Mr.Whippy was achieved through franchising the operation and, in this concept, Dominic would call on his experience at Meddocream and Neilsons. However, the emerging profitability of fleet operations meant that the business would continue to grow on two fronts, with company-owned vehicle numbers just exceeding the franchised operators by the end of the third year of trading.

Back at Chiswick, Ernest Pacitto was not developing his fleet in Mr.Whippy livery and it's understood that the London supply of Mr.Whippy ice cream mix was no longer coming from Mylo's, but Perfect Flavour Ice Cream in London's East End. In fact the Mr.Whippy van displayed at the Commercial Motor Show in the autumn of 1960 was in Mylo's livery. The Ice Cream Alliance takes up the story in April 1961: 'Some months ago, a division of interests took place. Mr Facchino wholly took over the Mr.Whippy side of the business; Mr Pacitto retained the Carpigiani agency and continues to concentrate on the manufacture of the vehicles used.'

The Mr.Whippy organisation continued its rapid growth during 1961, with company and franchised depots opening at quite a pace. Dominic thought, at this point, that a link-up with a large concern was desirable to promote his brand further. Negotiations with Northern Dairies were entered into and, as a result, the company took a 'substantial' interest in the Mr.Whippy organisation. Northern Dairies were certainly no strangers to Mr.Whippy, as they were already producing Mr.Whippy mix and running a fleet of 50 Mr.Whippy vans.

Although it's believed that Mr.Whippy got off to a slightly slower start than Mister Softee, the company stated that by August 1962, 800 vehicles were in operation nationwide. This published figure does seem a touch on the high side and it's suspected to be part of the age old tradition of 'advertisers puff'. An Ice Cream Alliance article in spring 1961, states that 150 Mr.Whippy vans were on the road with another 175 in the pipeline. Whatever the exact figures were, one thing was for certain, Mr.Whippy had now come of age and was emerging as a household name. A brand that subsequently became strong enough to slip silently into the English language.

This picture, taken in the mid-1960s, shows the Mr.Whippy fleet fuelling up ready for work. It's believed that there was a tie up with Esso at the time, as a plate on the generator's chassis stated 'Always use Esso Green TVO'. *Peter Hopkins*

Tractor Vaporising Oil

THIS was a common fuel when Mr.Whippy was launched back in 1959 and its use became an integral part of the daily life for a Mr.Whippy salesman in the 1960s and 1970s. With its distinctive smell, TVO fuelled the large 415V generators for up to 12 hours a day non-stop. TVO is part of a family of burning oils that includes paraffin, diesel and the oil used in domestic central heating boilers. TVO is a middle distillate premier grade burning oil (kerosene) with an improved aromatic content.

It was generally used in low compression spark ignition engines with a specially designed inlet manifold heat exchanger to vaporise the fuel, which had a very low octane number.No longer generally available, Aztec Oils Ltd of Bolsover is one of the few companies that still blend TVO in small quantities. Its formula is as follows: 75% kerosene+17% petrol+8% ISO 32 mineral oil. However, many of those who still run old TVO tractors, swear by their own particular formula.

When TVO became scarce in the latter half of the 1970s, some operators started using petrol to run their generators. This proved unsatisfactory and not just on the grounds of cost. Industrial — low compression — spark ignition engines designed to operate on TVO would not run as well on straight petrol. This would have resulted in some small loss of power, but more importantly the inefficient burning of the fuel would have caused the engine to run hotter than when TVO fuel was used. Replacing the head gasket to increase the compression ratio was one way to improve matters along with the fitting of a normal intake manifold and re-jetting of the carburettor. However, along with other factors, it was not long before the Commer/Karrier ice cream van with its TVO generator, became a rare sight and smell!

Mobile soft ice cream was once dominated by vans generating their own electricity via large TVO-fuelled generating sets. Pictured here is the largest of these which produced 12.5kVA of power at 415V. This powered two ice cream machines, the freezer, chiller cabinet, immersion heater and the van's 240V lighting.
Unilever

Coach-Built Vans

THE first Mr.Whippy vans were built on the Rootes Group forward-control 30cwt chassis by the coachbuilders, MTS of Feltham, West London. When returning from America in 1958, Dominic turned to business associate, Ernest Pacitto, with his idea for Mr.Whippy. Pacitto was not only the owner of Mylo's Ice Cream and agent for Carpigiani, he was also understood to have an interest in the Feltham coachbuilders at that time.

With Pacitto's experience in mobiling, the MTS-designed Mr.Whippy vans were ergonomically superior to Mister Softee vans, with the later production models just a touch quieter in operation. That's not to say that the prototype vans from both companies sailed through to production without any serious teething problems.

The problems encountered in those early days by Mister Softee were also mirrored at Mr.Whippy. This was mainly due to lack of engineering experience when bringing two technologies together for the first time in a mobile environment. A steep and sometimes painful learning curve was the order of the day. For example, the early industrial — belt driven — Coventry Victor powered 415V alternators in Mr.Whippy vans would only operate for a few hours before badly overheating. Mylo's were said to be running eight Whippy vans out of Hounslow and Facchino a further six, so a solution had to be found, and quickly! Enter A. C. Morrison Engineers Ltd of Southampton. Mylo's had contacted Morrisons for help, and a meeting was quickly set up between Stan Buchan of Morrisons, Ernest Pacitto and Dominic Facchino. Buchan saw the heart of the problem straight away. He described the heavy industrial Coventry Victor set-up as 'most unsuitable'. This was exacerbated by the cramped generator compartment and its poor ventilation.

Morrisons set to work and quickly designed a lighter in-line 12.5kVA generating set. An industrialised version of Ford's 1,703cc Consul engine was chosen, which would be fuelled by TVO. This sat on its own substantial chassis, which, in turn, was bolted to the vehicle chassis via rubber mountings. A specially designed radiator and fan were also employed.

Time was of the essence and the new generators were quickly fitted into the existing and poorly ventilated compartments. However, after some teething problems, the generator compartments were redesigned and then incorporated into production vehicles at MTS in Feltham. Back at Southampton, Morrisons were also retrofitting Mister Softee vans with new generating sets in order to overcome the same overheating problems encountered by Mr.Whippy.

To ensure continuity of vehicle supply, anecdotal evidence suggests that MTS coachbuilders were quickly taken over by Dominic Facchino and Ernest Pacitto for

Mr.Whippy chose the tried and tested Commer/Karrier forward-control chassis from the Rootes Group. This advert, *circa* 1961, is similar to one showing that the rival Mister Softee organisation had also chosen the same chassis to build their vans.

All the early Mr.Whippy vans were hand-painted in pink and cream coach enamel. Here we see, in the 1963 MTS brochure, craftsmen painting the last of the Commer/Karrier models that, for the first time, had a rear window and a forward-facing, rear-mounted ice cream machine.

Mr. Whippy chooses
KARRIER
1 TONNERS

The illustration shows one of the fleet of Karrier 1 ton mobile ice cream shops supplied to Mr.Whippy (Soft Freeze) Ltd., of Leamington Spa.

Easily handled in crowded streets and narrow spaces, yet large enough to carry substantial loads, the Karrier 1 ton forward control van is the choice of a growing number of operators who want a reliable, economical vehicle that will stand up to the exacting demands of 'stop-start' delivery work. Built to the highest quality standards, with a lively 4 cylinder petrol or diesel engine the Karrier 1 tonner is available with an attractive all-steel van body of 280 cu. ft. capacity. Alternatively the chassis will accommodate specially designed bodies to suit individual requirements, the above being a striking example of its usage.

BUILT STRONGER TO LAST LONGER!

KARRIER MOTORS LTD. LUTON BEDFORDSHIRE   EXPORT DIVISION: ROOTES LTD. DEVONSHIRE HOUSE PICCADILLY LONDON W.1

Although Mr.Whippy vans were predominantly built on Commer/Karrier chassis in the early years, some other chassis were also used. Here we see what is believed to be a 'Sparshatts'-built van on an Austin LD chassis commissioned by Mr.Whippy agents, Northern Dairies. *Ice Cream Alliance.*

It's not clear what the exact relationship between MTS and Electrofreeze was. What we do know is that, while Facchino's new Electrofreeze company was producing Mr.Whippy vans in Southampton, MTS were still involved with van production, as this 1963 MTS brochure clearly shows. Dominic Facchino in winter 1963 was still shown as a director of MTS.

the sole purpose of building soft ice cream vans. Like Mister Softee vans — built by Smiths — these vans were extremely expensive, but certainly not exclusive to Mr.Whippy franchise holders. A fully-fitted Commer would set an operator back a cool £3,400 or a slightly reduced price of £3,200 if you were a Whippy franchise holder. As orders for Whippy vans increased and pressure placed on the West London production, it's understood that a number of bodies were also constructed, with detailed differences, by Bonnalacks of Basildon, Essex.

It's not clear how the relationship between Facchino and Pacitto developed, or whether the relationship in fact terminated altogether. One thing, however, is for sure, Mylo's clearly decided not to continue with the Mr.Whippy brand. Dominic Facchino was certainly concerned about the situation and continuity of vehicle supply continued to be uppermost in his mind. He again turned to Stan Buchan at Morrisons.

As a result a meeting was set up between the Morrisons board, Stan Buchan and Dominic Facchino to discuss the proposal that Morrisons should take on Mr.Whippy van production. The idea of ice cream van production 'left them all cold' said Buchan, who was in favour of the proposition. Facchino was a determined man and, not to be thwarted, asked Buchan if he would consider taking over production and design under a newly-formed company.

After 10 years with Morrisons it was not an easy decision, but Buchan agreed and, as a result, Electrofreeze was born — a name thought up by Buchan that soon gave him 'strife' with the American Electrofreeze Inc. A company was later incorporated in July 1960 as Electrofreeze (Equipments) Ltd. The new company initially started by only equipping the MTS-built bodies. However, production of Mr.Whippy vans was soon underway at the Southampton facility, under the name Electrofreeze (Southampton) Ltd.

This period shot shows the interior of the MkIII model that is featured on our front cover. The roof lining was painted pegboard with blue gingham Formica surfaces. The white walls were made from Swedish Royal Board. *Peter Hopkins*

It's been said that once full vehicle production at Electrofreeze was up and running, all Mr.Whippy van production was transferred to this new company. However, a recent discovery of a 1963 MTS brochure, clearly shows the new Electrofreeze designed (1962/5) model) being built at MTS. This is further underlined by a 1963 letter showing Dominic Facchino as being on the MTS board of directors.

The first Mr.Whippy vans on the 30cwt chassis weighed-in at well over three tons, but had features that made them arguably better to operate than the lighter Softee vans. Unlike Softee vans, the driving seat swivelled 180 degrees clockwise via a foot-operated pedal. This allowed the driver the easiest of access to the serving area. It also avoided much swearing and personal injury, as it wasn't necessary to climb over the hand brake and gear lever a hundred times a day.

The production vans also had an offside floor-to-roof side-opening door in the serving area. This made life so much easier for washing out the vehicle and the loading and unloading of stock. An added benefit on production models, up to 1962, was the ability to secure this door to the rear bodywork when fully open. A boon when pitching up on those hot summer days. However, taller drivers would no doubt have been envious of the extra headroom afforded to Mister Softee drivers.

Arguably, the early production model Mr.Whippy vans were better served by their larger 12.5kVA, three-phase (415V) generators. The extra 5kVA of power, compared to Softee vans, allowed the use of a twin-barrelled Carpigiani machine, or two single machines. The most commonly used generator power unit was Ford's robust 1,703cc industrial version of the Consul/Zephyr engine. At 1,500rpm, it ran 300rpm slower than a Softee generator and, therefore, was just a touch quieter.

However, it wasn't long before the expensive and very heavy twin-barrelled machines were dropped in favour of a single pump-fed machine. This allowed the smaller and cheaper — 7.5kVA Ford 102E side-valve — generator sets to be used. The new pump-fed machines were capable of producing more ice cream per hour than the earlier drip-fed models and kept up well with long queues. This reduced the overall weight and therefore allowed the use of the 12in shorter — and cheaper — 20cwt Commer/Karrier chassis. This, in turn, significantly reduced the on-the-road cost to a figure in the region of £2,500.

Built by Roach Trailers of Ower, the Morrison Electrofreeze 'Powerdrive' model is the only known ice cream van to have a unique chassis commissioned by an ice cream coachbuilder. *Peter Hopkins*

Morrison Electrofreeze of Southampton pioneered the use of 'one-piece' GRP ice cream van coachwork. Today this method is still the industry standard.

The Rootes Group Bantam forward-control chassis was robust and fully suited being used for ice cream coachwork, where good interior space was required. It also coped with the weight of a large generator and twin ice cream machines. *Rootes Group*

This Electrofreeze CA Bedford was first registered to Tartaglia's in 1965. Mike Allen of Tartaglia's says it was a prototype van with much of the panelwork made of aluminium, unlike the later all GRP-bodied models. *Unilever*

Space was, however, slightly compromised; this led to the single 'clock-face' Carpigiani ice cream machine being moved a few inches forward into the driver's compartment. However, little useable space was lost by this 12in reduction in chassis length, and most drivers said they were easier to drive.

Yet, this model was only to be a stop-gap measure. Electrofreeze was now producing Mr.Whippy vans and looking to improve the design and, I should imagine, cut costs.

Stan Buchan and his team soon realised that internal space could be much better utilised within the one-ton chassis models.

A new layout was conceived for the 1962 season and a prototype vehicle designed. However, the construction of the first pre-production van was undertaken by 'Picador', the neighbouring Southampton builder of tonibell vans. For some strange reason this van did not go to Mr.Whippy, but to a Bristol mobiler, Colin Tarr. The only proviso was that it could not be painted Pink & Cream.

The upper space in the generator compartment was now incorporated into the main serving area of the van, and, for the first time, a rear window introduced. The depth of the generator compartment increased to accommodate a side-by-side engine alternator configuration. The single 'clock-face' Carpigiani ice cream machine now sat centrally over the generator compartment facing forward. The freezer and chiller compartment — for the ice cream mix — were now located at the front nearside. The sink now sat neatly under the ice cream machine.

This new configuration not only increased internal space, it may have just slightly lightened the load on the front axle. Although a distinct improvement over the old model, in terms of space and rearward visibility, some drivers didn't like switching to serving customers the opposite way round. It's interesting to note that virtually all-modern vans have the ice cream machine facing rearwards. It's understood that all export models from 1962 were of this final layout until Commer BF production ceased in 1965.

Back at the start of production in 1959, the Commer/Karrier vans were fitted out with grey and white Formica surfaces, which later gave way to the now familiar blue and white gingham design. The interior roof lining was made from pegboard and the white wipe clean wall surfaces were made of Swedish 'Royal Board'. The gingham Formica surfaces were used throughout the production life of Mr.Whippy Commer/Karriers.

It is said that the first van was fitted with two 10-gallon water tanks, one of which supplied hot water via a gravity-fed 240V immersion heater. However, the author's two 1961 examples had only one hot supply fitted. The early drip-fed Carpigiani machines were capable of producing up to seven gallons of ice cream per hour with a very modest 40% overrun. This, of course, would have been a considerably lower air to mix ratio than the later pump-fed machines. Today, the public are used to 'fluffy' soft ice cream from mobiles. Back in 1960, soft ice cream had substance, which was evident from the weight of the cornets.

These vans had a capacity of keeping up to 32-gallons of fresh mix chilled, while the non-holdover cabinet — the freezer — was quite small by today's standards. Stock either had to be removed to a cold room overnight or the van plugged into the mains to operate the freezer. Each van had two full-length internal fluorescent strip lights, and one external over the serving window. This made Whippy vans very attractive at night, and quite useful when you consider that soft ice cream vans were so popular in those early years that working profitably during the dark winter evenings was possible.

The Electrofreeze team in Southampton, then turned its attention to the development of a 15cwt model on the popular Bedford CA chassis with prototypes probably on the road well before Commer production came to an end. The new Glass Reinforced Plastic (GRP) bodied models had three distinctive body styles and were made from many individual GRP mouldings fabricated by Wincanton Engineering. These new models also dispensed with Bedford's steel front end.

The heavy side-by-side 7.5kVA generator set was said to have been initially carried over to the 15cwt chassis. However, I have my doubts, as this would surely have pushed the on-the-road weight well over its limit. The much lighter Onan generator was also known to have been fitted and was probably an option for production models.

It is understood that several other ways of powering the ice cream machine were tried, one of these being the use of a slave engine located in the generator compartment. A 'Velocette' water-cooled engine was employed to provide the motive power via electro-magnetic clutches. This configuration was, however, not developed further.

These developments at Electrofreeze were at a time when S. C. Cummins of Crewe was already in production with its yet to be patented 'Direct Drive' technology. This was a system that simply eradicated the need for a secondary power source for the ice cream machine.

The idea of 'direct drive' to power the ice cream machine was not a new concept. At the Ice Cream Alliance Exhibition in 1961, Walter Relph Ltd exhibited a 'direct-drive ice cream freezer', which was fitted to two vans at the Scarborough show. However, in 1962 Bryan Whitby at S. C. Cummins developed a system that soon became the industry standard and is still in use today throughout the world.

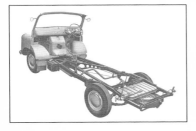

From its introduction, the Bedford CA was much favoured by the ice cream trade. As a soft ice cream van in the early 1960s it struggled with the weight penalty of a generator and ice cream machine. This was all to change when 'Direct drive' technology did away with the need for an onboard mains generation plant.

Electrofreeze, in the meantime, had been taken over by Morrison Industries, the very company that had previously turned up their noses at being involved with ice cream van production. The demise of the CA and the introduction of Bedford's all-new CF model in 1969 came as rather a surprise to Morrison Electrofreeze and, therefore, left it in a difficult situation. It very quickly had to develop a new body for the CF to meet demand from customers such as Wall's-Whippy and Mister Softee who had moved away from Smiths-built vans. At this point Stan Buchan, the Managing Director, considered a quick fix via a return to a traditional coachbuilt body. However, Morrison's chief engineer, Terry Newman, was convinced that a one-piece GRP body was the only way forward.

Buchan listened and agreed, the only proviso being that Newman had to produce a design that did not require a conventional interior lining throughout the vehicle structure. This resulted in producing what many mobilers say was one of the finest vans of its day. The proof of the pudding is always in the eating, and over the decades these Morrison Electrofreeze bodies were removed and mounted onto newer chassis. This bodyshell was also modified to fit the Ford Transit which was fast becoming more popular with mobilers.

With the introduction of the CF model, Morrisons looked to the 'Direct Drive' system developed by Bryan Whitby as the only practical way of powering the ice cream equipment. A pulley-type electro-magnetic clutch was mounted on the vehicle's engine to supply the motive power. The machine stayed in the Morrisons' preferred position at the rear of the vehicle, facing forward. This necessitated the use of an RDG (reverse drive gearbox) machine, which enabled the equipment to turn in the right direction. The driver had a red lever, which, when depressed, lifted the engine's speed and activated a switch to engage the electro-magnetic clutches. Later on, a rear-facing, front-mounted machine was introduced, and, therefore, available to the now fully franchised Wall's-Whippy operation.

There was one other important development at Morrison Electrofreeze, and it is well worth a mention here. When Vauxhall-Bedford axed the CA chassis, it left the Southampton company with a significant stock of bodies that couldn't be mounted onto the new chassis. Enter the Morrisons patented 'Powerdrive' model built on a new chassis by Roach Trailers of Ower. Although Mr.Whippy did not purchase these new, some second-hand examples were believed to have found their way into Mr.Whippy livery.

This new model employed a power take-off from the gearbox via a 'Simplitrol' electro-magnetic clutch. This, in turn, drove a shaft and pulley arrangement to rotate the 12kVA 415V generator in the rear. This was all activated via a secondary, ignition type, key on the dashboard. This arrangement, designed by Ted Maynard, fed power to the solenoid and magnetic clutch, which. in turn. engaged the engine's governor. The 1:1 gearing from the van's Ford 1,600 cross-flow unit meant that the governor kept the engine speed to 1,500rpm.

Most other parts were sourced from the Ford Transit which is why people think that this 'Powerdrive' model is based on a Ford Transit chassis. Some of these unique vans have survived including several in the United States.

Empire Building

With Mr.Whippy now firmly established, Dominic Facchino defined his companies' aims as:

- The building and selling of Ice cream vehicles;
- Mr.Whippy as a franchised operation;
- Company-owned Mr.Whippy fleet operations.

These were heady days for all involved in what was fast becoming an ice cream empire. Peter Hopkins, who can best be described as Dominic Facchino's right-hand-man, particularly remembers those early years of 'empire building' with great affection: 'Dominic Facchino was, in my opinion, a great man, who enthused us all with his vitality and vision for the future. It was of course hard work and long hours, but we did feel that we were part of something special, and that was quite exciting.'

Once established, Mr.Whippy quickly entered into a period of acquisitions, partnerships and expansion through the formation of new companies. As we have seen on the vehicle building side, Facchino was not completely happy with the way things were going at MTS in Feltham, so he set up Electrofreeze in Southampton with Stan Buchan and his partners, Ted Maynard and Geoff Goodwin, with Mr.Whippy holding a 50% share in this new company.

By spring 1961, with over 150 Mr.Whippy vans on the road and Facchino's involvement in numerous companies, it was felt that an umbrella company should be formed. On 28 April 1961, Mr.Whippy (Holdings) Ltd was formed, with Mr.Whippy Ltd, Mr.Whippy (Softfreeze) Ltd, Mr.Whippy (Tyne) Ltd, Mr.Whippy (Scotland) Ltd, Electrofreeze (Equipments) Ltd, and the Soft Ice Cream Co Ltd all coming under its wing as would subsequent Whippy companies.

Dominic soon turned his attention to the production of ice cream mix, as the pasteurised mix was being produced to the same recipe by companies in the Midlands, Hull and London. It was felt that Mr.Whippy should not be dependent on these outside suppliers and, therefore, decided to commence production of ice cream mix in-house. To this end, negotiations to purchase its London supplier were entered into. On 21 August 1961, Perfect Flavour Ice Cream Co Ltd became another Mr.Whippy acquisition, with MD and major shareholder A. E. Pellosi remaining in day-to-day charge of the company.

Expansion during 1961 was in stark contrast to 1960 when all but six new Mr.Whippy vans were owned by franchise holders. Company-operated depots now began to emerge and, along with new franchise holders, Mr.Whippy was now close

This rather evocative picture was taken in Australia shortly after the successful launch of Mr.Whippy down under in 1962. Note the Sundae dispenser and the hot water tap now located under the rear-mounted Carpigiani ice cream machine. *Peter Hopkins*

The first Mr.Whippy ice cream parlour was opened at Whitley Bay in 1962 by Edwin Thirlwell, Managing Director of the Tyne Ice Cream Co and Mr.Whippy (Tyne) Ltd. *Peter Hopkins*

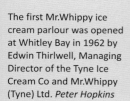

to being able to boast a truly national presence. By the end of 1961, some 360 Mr.Whippy vans — all being Commer/Karriers — were said to be on the road whilst several company depots were now up and running (with more scheduled for 1962). From the outset, the company had enjoyed a strong presence in London and the Midlands, but with depots such as Gateshead, Swansea, Welwyn Garden City, Tipton, Manchester and Paisley, the Mr.Whippy brand was established as a truly national player, and one that the 'big boys' could no longer ignore.

To continue this rapid expansion through the later part of 1961 and into 1962, Dominic negotiated to sell a 50% interest in Mr.Whippy (Softfreeze) Ltd, the owners of the Mr.Whippy franchise, to Northern Dairies Ltd. This was completed on 1 August 1961 and gave the Mr.Whippy group an important association with a publicly-quoted company.

By the end of 1961, Mr.Whippy had started to gain great momentum, and its confidence in the future as a big player in mobiling was felt to be assured. By 1962, Electrofreeze in Southampton was turning out vans as fast as it could make them, as new franchise-holders continued to join the Mr.Whippy family and with the growth of company-owned depots continuing at a rapid pace. By the summer of 1962 there were said to be 24 company depots and 48 franchise depots. That year was set to be an extremely hectic year for Dominic and certain key personnel, notably Peter Hopkins and the group chief accountant, Roy Robertson.

On 13 January 1962, Mr.Whippy (Holdings) Ltd acquired from Dominic Facchino and Northern Dairies their shares in Mr.Whippy (Soft freeze) Ltd, which was the owners of the Mr.Whippy franchise. Each party received 50,000 shares in Mr.Whippy (Holdings) Ltd.

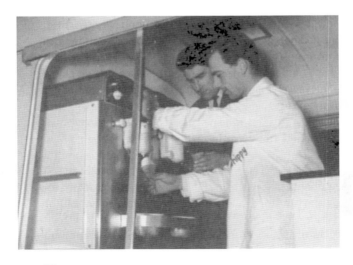

Training was a key part of the Mr.Whippy philosophy as shown here in a company photo from the publication *Frozen Assets. Peter Hopkins*

Today only a very few original Mr.Whippy vans survive. Here we see the author's van being used on a video shoot in the 1990s with the the Tennant brothers — aka The Pet Shop Boys. *Gary Sutton.*

On 31 January 1962 Dominic Facchino bought from Northern Dairies 24,000 shares in Mr.Whippy (Holdings) Ltd. This increased Dominic's personal holding in the company to 74%, leaving Northern Dairies with the remaining 26%.

Having purchased the Perfect Flavour company the previous year, the Group now undertook to build a 'state of the art' ice cream factory on a new two-acre site at Basildon in Essex. The factory cost £250,000 and had a production capacity of three million gallons of ice cream mix per annum. The new factory, run by A. E Pelosi, was fully automated and came into production on 1 July 1962. The plant also produced ice cream and ice-lollies and boasted one of only two American-built Vitaline production units to be installed in the UK. At this time a further six specially designed — five- and seven-ton — refrigerated vehicles were purchased to supply bulk loads to the growing family of Mr.Whippy depots.

The rapid expansion of Mr.Whippy and the group's profitability led Dominic, in the early part of 1962, to consider a public floatation. It was during these negotiations that Dominic Facchino and Charles Forte used to meet at the Cafe Royal Sporting Club in London. Over their many informal chats about their respective companies, the topic of the floatation of Mr.Whippy arose. Dominic had obviously whetted Mr Forte's appetite during these informal chats and, as a consequence it was decided to suspend any proposals for a floatation and enter into serious negotiations with the Forte Group. During summer 1962 an agreement

Left: By the end of 1962 there were 735 Mr.Whippy vans operating from 79 depots in England, Wales, Scotland and Northern Ireland. Pictured here are the company-owned depots at Manchester (top), Gateshead and Tipton. *Peter Hopkins*

Below: This rather poor photograph, taken in Rotherham in the early 1960s, is included as it clearly shows the American influence with the use of forage caps and bow ties. *Peter Hopkins*

was reached between the parties. It was agreed that Mr.Whippy (Holdings) Ltd would amalgamate with the Forte's (Holdings) Ltd on 11 October 1962.

Prior to these negotiations being completed by the two companies, Dominic had agreed to sell 23% of his personal shareholding in Mr.Whippy (Holdings) Ltd to Charles Forte. So, at the point of amalgamation, Dominic Facchino held 51%, Northern Dairies 26% and Charles Forte 23%. At the Forte floatation, Dominic Facchino, Northern Dairies and Charles Forte sold their holdings in Mr.Whippy to the Forte group. The transaction being as follows:

- ■ Dominic Facchino — 51,000 shares — consideration — 1 million Forte shares;
- ■ Northern Dairies — 26,000 shares — consideration— 350,000 Forte shares;
- ■ Charles Forte (Nominees) — 23,000 shares — consideration — 309,617 Forte shares.

With the value of Forte shares set at £1, this obviously made Dominic Facchino a very happy man and, of course, the newest member of the millionaire club. Not bad in just over three and a half years of operation. At the point of floatation there were 735 Mr.Whippy vans on the road and, from this number, 374 were owned and operated from company depots. At this stage, there were 23 company depots operated by various companies in the group and 56 depots run by franchised agents.

I think it was fair to say that as 1962 came to a close, there was no doubt that Mr.Whippy ice cream could be bought in every densely populated area of England and Wales, with strong inroads being made north of the border, through Mr.Whippy (Scotland) Ltd. This was also the year that saw the Mr.Whippy brand leave our shores for sunnier climes. However, this may never have happened, if it were not for a chance meeting — in a hotel bar — between Dominic Facchino and a Mr Bill Kendell, an ice cream operator from Sydney, on holiday in England.

On August Bank Holiday Monday 1962 a meeting took place between Dominic Facchino, key members of his staff and Mr Bill Kendell. Arising from this was an agreement to start a Mr.Whippy operation in Australia. Peter Hopkins, who was present throughout, said: 'It was incredible to think that we had only one meeting with Bill Kendell. We were all very enthusiastic, we shook hands, drew up an agreement and simply went away and made it happen. In fact, we had 10 Mr.Whippy vans on board a ship (at Southampton docks) bound for Sydney the very next month. Those were certainly exciting days.'

The Australian company— Mr.Whippy PTY Ltd — was formed with a capital of 35,001 Australian pounds. Mr.Whippy (Holdings) Ltd held technical control with 17,501 shares, while Bill Kendell, the new company's MD, held 17,500. The first batch of vans arrived at Sydney Docks and were unloaded on 22 October 1962. These were all short-wheelbase models and were the first and last Commer/Karrier vans designed by Electrofreeze.

ICE CREAM & FROZEN CONFECTIONERY. MARCH, 1962

Treat Products, the well-known Leeds firm, became part of the Mr.Whippy organisation for a short period before being sold back to its former owners. This advert shows the company had a wide range of products that it sold mainly to the independent sector. *Ice Cream Alliance*

The first Mr.Whippy depot in Australia was at Rockdale with four of the 10 vans working the streets of Sydney within four days of their arrival. Whilst negotiations with Forte were at their height during summer 1962, Dominic was invited to bid for a major share in another well known ice cream brand.

This company, called Treat Products of Leeds, was mainly involved in supplying the independent sector with a wide range of wrapped products. Ron Peters of tonibell already had an offer on the table to purchase 60% of Treat and, therefore, Dominic needed to move quickly. However, negotiations with Forte and other pressing matters precluded Dominic's personal involvement, so negotiations were entrusted to two key members of his staff. The outcome was successful with 80% of Treat being acquired by Mr.Whippy (Holdings) Ltd for a sum in the region of £180,000.

However, this acquisition was extremely sensitive at the time and was, therefore, kept very quiet. For years independent mobilers had been buying their products from Treat, and would have not been too happy about buying their stock from the very people they were in competition with out on the streets. For this reason, it is believed that a special dispensation was given to leave this acquisition out of the Forte/Whippy prospectus. However, Mr.Whippy's holding in Treat was short-lived and subsequently sold back to its former owners prior to Whippy's involvement with Wall's.

It was also a busy year for Dominic's brother Anthony, who had secured the contract to produce Mr.Whippy cones from his new factory— The Cake Cone Co — in Tamworth, Staffordshire, in 1962. By the end of 1963, Anthony's company was boasting that it was 'one of the largest producers of cones in Great Britain — manufacturing at a steady rate of over 20 million cones a month'. Whether or not this was exactly true, the company was certainly busy producing vast numbers of cones bearing the Mr.Whippy brand name. In fact, as demand rose, the company's order book soon became dependent on Mr.Whippy. As a consequence, full production capacity was soon turned over to Mr.Whippy in order to meet the growing demand from the expanding network of company and franchise depots throughout the country.

The Facchino family business was famous for making cones and wafers. After the launch of Mr.Whippy, Anthony Facchino returned to what he knew best and formed the The Cake Cone Co in Tamworth. which supplied cones to his brother's Mr.Whippy organisation. The delivery fleet used BMC FG box vans with the 'three-penny bit' cab. *Ice Cream Alliance*

In 1962 Mr.Whippy built a state-of-the-art ice cream factory in Basildon, Essex which was run by Mr A. E. Pelosi. Unfortunately, within just a few short years, the plant became a casualty of rationalisation after the formation of Wall's-Whippy. *Peter Hopkins*

The Forte Years

As Mr.Whippy entered 1963 as an integral part of the Forte Empire, there seemed to be little day-to-day evidence of change. The Forte broom had obviously not felt the need to sweep clean and clearly demonstrated the faith that Charles Forte had put in Dominic Facchino and his team. Dominic, therefore, remained as Chairman and Managing Director (with a lucrative seven-year contract), and Peter Hopkins continued as General Manager.

On paper the deal looked good, Mr.Whippy had demonstrated a healthy profitability in the previous two years, and Forte clearly believed that the best way forward was to keep a winning team at the helm. However, this faith was not to be rewarded, as the financial success of Mr.Whippy was not to continue under the Forte umbrella. Charles Forte would soon learn that all was not rosy in the Whippy garden, as trading losses soon became evident. A source close to Charles Forte said: 'Charles felt rather let down by Dominic and his team. He clearly felt that they had taken their eye off the ball after the amalgamation. In fact he rued the day he got involved!'

In Charles Forte's biography, he clearly states this to be the case when looking back to his involvement with Mr.Whippy: 'Our accountants studied the figures and recommended the purchase. I was also impressed by the Chairman and Managing Director of the company. But I had made a mistake. As soon as I bought the company, the management seemed to lose a lot of interest and it was not long before Mr.Whippy was losing a lot of money.'

In fact, losses would amount to £500,000, which in 2003 prices would be well over £5 million. Forte went on to say: 'It was a complete failure and in many ways a salutary experience. It proved to us that we were by no means infallible. It also taught me a lesson — never acquire a business however good it may appear to be, unless you are either guaranteed continuity of management, or you are in a position to replace the management.'

It's not quite clear what Forte meant here by 'continuity of management', as both managing director and general manager remained at the helm of

Charles Forte regularly met with Dominic Facchino at London's Cafe Royal Sporting Club and these informal meetings led the two men to agree that Mr.Whippy would join the Forte Group. The amalgamation took place in October 1962 and as a result made Dominic Facchino a millionaire. *Peter Hopkins*

Forte was no stranger to the ice cream business as this picture demonstrates. Taken in 1958 the vehicle is a Vespa scooter — probably a 125cc model. *Ice Cream Alliance*

After the amalgamation between Forte and Wall's of the Mr.Whippy brand, economies of scale were presented to the company — one notable area was in the use of central maintenance units, as seen here in the main Wall's workshops. *Unilever*

33

Sell it as 'Wallsiwhip' and you
get all the advantages of a nation-
ally-advertised soft ice cream. Also,
bulk buying enables Wall's to
offer you leading makes of freezers
at generous discounts—and there
are special hire purchase facilities
available. Plus a free initial supply
of 24 cans of Wall's sterile liquid
mix! For further information ring
your local Wall's depot or the Sales
Manager, T. Wall & Sons (Ice Cream)
Ltd., Barnwood Road, Gloucester.
Telephone Gloucester 21521.

Sell it under your own
brand name!

Sell it and you'll profit—
like this:

Order	Standard Quality per can	Dairy Quality per can
1–24 cans	12/-	15/-
25–294 cans	11/6	14/6
295 cans plus	11/-	14/-

These outlays will yield between
30/- and 45/- per can.

There's a world
of difference
in a Wall's

Wall's
ICE CREAM

FIRST
in
FLAVOUR

When Wall's developed 'Wallsiwhipp' in 1963, the writing was on the wall for Mr.Whippy's own 'mix production' facility in Essex. In 1964, after the formation of Wall's-Whippy Ltd, the standard quality canned 'Wallsiwhipp' soon replaced the original Mr.Whippy recipe. *Ice Cream Alliance*

Mr.Whippy throughout the Forte period and beyond. The situation in 1963 was clearly not helped by the recent imposition of Purchase Tax on ice cream and the worst winter the country had seen since 1947. However, to the general public, Mr.Whippy was a great success and fast becoming a household name. In spite of its losses the brand was set to embark on another phase of its life that spanned from the late 1950s through the 1960s, 1970s and overseas into the 21st century.

The company may have been losing serious money, but to the drivers and franchise holders this was the heyday of soft ice cream mobiling, and sales by today's standards were extremely high. Michael Lloyd, whose father Peter ran the 20-strong Leamington Spa depot, said: 'In those days it was not unusual to get through 30-gallons of mix a day. On one particular occasion, I can clearly remember pulling onto a housing estate and not having to move all day. Modern mobilers would find that extremely hard to believe, but it's true.'

During the summer of 1963 Charles Forte and Wall's started negotiations, as Wall's had clearly missed the boat with regard to its own involvement with soft ice cream mobiling and was keen to regain lost ground. Although Wall's was already running a limited number of soft ice cream vans, the company had failed to react to the early success and subsequent rapid growth of the Mister Softee and Mr.Whippy brands.

It would be fair to say that Wall's was not alone here in its sluggish response, because many others in the trade were in denial concerning the success (and, therefore, longevity) of soft ice cream mobiling during the early 1960s. Of the larger fleet operators, only tonibell seemed to be making the wholesale transition to soft serve ice cream. Wall's, therefore, saw in Mr.Whippy not only an opportunity to catch up quickly, but also the chance to eliminate a competitor in a market sector that it now needed to take more seriously. By the end of the summer of 1963, an agreement had been reached and a joint venture company would soon merge the Wall's mobiling operation with Mr.Whippy.

This arrangement would later be known as Wall's-Whippy Ltd, and was to be a partnership of equals, with management and financial control jointly shared between Wall's and Forte. The number of directors would be increased from three to six to reflect the new structure, with three directors being appointed by Wall's and three from Forte. The official launch of this new joint venture was on 1 January 1964, although the company name was not changed until 27 January. The company — now renamed Wall's-Whippy Ltd —continued to operate from the Mr.Whippy headquarters at Warwick House, Leamington Spa.

Dominic Facchino remained as MD whilst Mr J. Knowles (Wall's) was appointed Chairman and Mr J. Kinlock (Wall's direct selling) joined Peter Hopkins as Joint General Manager. The new joint venture company now boasted a mixed fleet of some 1,800 vans, with about 1,000 of these being soft serve. Wall's had approximately 150 soft vans in their fleet, which were soon re-painted in Mr.Whippy livery at a cost of £30 per vehicle. Chimes were also changed to Greensleeves at a cost of £12 each. Wall's was now to supply tinned sterile mix to Wall's-Whippy at an agreed transportation cost of 3d per tin. Wall's wrapped products were now available on all Mr.Whippy vans, although this was rather restricted by the poor size of the freezer cabinet in the Commer/Karrier fleet.

In 1964, regular Mr.Whippy customers — with discerning palates — would have noticed a change in their ice cream, when the Mr.Whippy Ice Cream mix was replaced by Wall's standard canned sterile mix. The new Wall's liquid mix, introduced in 1963, was called 'Wallsiwhip' and came in both Dairy and Standard form. The Mr.Whippy driver who came down our street at the time said that 'the customers much preferred the old recipe, but in time everyone got used to the new flavour'.

On a few occasions Mr.Whippy made it into the movies, most notably with the opening and closing sequences of the *Sandwich Board Man* starring Michael Bentine. Another use in film of a Mr.Whippy van is seen here in the baddies' mode of transport in the Beatles' film *Help*. *Photo courtesy of Walter Shenson Pictures*

Although this picture is of a very poor quality, it clearly shows the rebranding of several MkI Bedford CAs to Mr.Whippy livery following the coming together of Wall's Ice Cream and Mr.Whippy. *Unilever*

Early Mr.Whippy vans used a twin 'drip-fed' machine and later on two single 'pump-fed' machines. To reduce costs the 30cwt chassis was dropped in favour of a 20cwt chassis and a single Carpigiani machine, identical to the one pictured here. *Unilever*

Changes at Mr.Whippy were not without their casualties, as Peter Hopkins recalls: 'We had a new "state of the art" ice cream factory in Basildon, which would no longer be required, if Wall's joined with us. By late summer of 1963 the deal with Wall's was finalised in principal, and I knew what that would mean for our Basildon factory. Aturo Pelosi was our Chief Executive at the factory as well as a close friend. I had the unenviable task of travelling to Essex to break the news that his factory was to be closed and therefore he, and his staff, would be out of a job. That was tough!' The Basildon factory was eventually taken over by Rains Dairies Ltd.

Opposite: This interesting picture was taken just after the formation of Wall's-Whippy in 1964 and shows a Wall's Morris LD rebranded in Mr.Whippy livery, but with no soft ice cream machine fitted. As Mr.Whippy was a purely a soft ice cream brand, this all seems very strange. *Unilever*

Above left: The lower image is a rare, if rather poor, picture of a prototype Mr.Whippy boat-style trailer designed for static operation. The trailer had its own generator and Carpigiani machine. The picture above shows a static trailer at one of Forte's motorway service areas. Note the American Sweden Freeze machine. *Peter Hopkins*

Above right: Rather large by today's standards, the early long-wheel-base Mr.Whippy vans had a fully laden weight of just over 3.5 tons. *Peter Hopkins*

The Wall's-Whippy Years

I T all sounded so simple: two leading brands with complimentary fleets, each having a national network of depots. Put them together to form Wall's-Whippy Ltd, what could be easier — 'a reasonably intelligent three year old could do it!' Wrong! First of all, no one was quite sure where all the vans were, then came the fact that the depots were either too large, too small, in the wrong place or even worse, didn't even exist. The majority of district and depot managers lived long distances from where they were needed and, to cap it all, Easter 1964 fell very early in the year, and ice cream sales were very poor. Many wished they hadn't entered into the joint venture....!

The objective was to integrate the 1,500 plus combined fleet of hard and soft vans into both Wall's and Whippy depots at a ratio of somewhere in the region of 24 hard (wrapped) to 16 soft vans. The result proved that a total rethink would have to be the order of the day. Chaos ensued and the new Head Office even struggled to provide basic services in many areas.

Existing Wall's managers were seconded to the new Wall's-Whippy depots to act on a number 1/number 2 basis, but many who found themselves demoted to the number 2 position predictably found other jobs. Several former Wall's personnel were also disaffected by what they saw as their 'New parentless status' and opted for self-employment under the Wall's-Whippy umbrella.

The next two years saw a great deal of change and, after the initial chaos, during and after the birth of Wall's-Whippy Ltd, a new optimism began to grow — albeit slowly — as the rationalisation and integration of the two fleets and depots became a workable reality. On the franchise front, new agents were continuing to join the brand in encouraging numbers. However, it soon became clear that the emphasis of Wall's-Whippy would have to move in the direction of a wholly franchised operation.

An entrepreneurial atmosphere was soon created as many ex-depot managers, senior personnel and selected van drivers were encouraged to take on a franchise operation. It's not clear exactly when Wall's-Whippy finances moved into the black, but the decision to move away from company-owned depots and relaunch as a fully-franchised operation was certainly a key factor in their future success.

At the end of 1963, prior to amalgamation, Wall's direct selling fleet consisted of 147 soft ice cream vans, 499 wrapped vans and 363 of the smaller 'minivans' such as the left-hand-drive Ford Thames 7cwt. Of these, 611 operated under the new Wall's-Whippy company for the 1964 season. Some vans from the Wall's fleet, such as the Trojans, were deemed to be too old to join the new combined fleet! Furthermore, some Wall's depots, with a wholesale operation, were also excluded from the new joint venture.

This line-up of pretty Electrofreeze Bedford CAs is seen here at the 1968 Ice Cream Alliance exhibition at Buxton.
Ice Cream Alliance

Although Wall's was rather slow off the mark with regard to mobile soft ice cream, it did in fact run soft ice cream vans. Here we see a Bedford CA fitted with a Carpigiani machine powered by an LPG fuelled Onan generator.
Stuart Whitby

Wall's-Whippy introduced the 'Good Humor' brand in an attempt to compete with Lyons' premium 'Napoli' brand. This mobile concept was not, however, a great success! *Peter Hopkins*

Later, the full amalgamation of the Mr.Whippy and Wall's mobiling fleets would create an estimated 1,800-strong mixed fleet — almost certainly the largest in the country. Of these about 1,000 would be selling soft ice cream, branded in Mr.Whippy colours, whilst the remainder continued in the traditional blue and cream Wall's livery.

Whilst Mr.Whippy continued to make good profits for drivers and franchised depots, Wall's-Whippy Ltd as a whole was far less fortunate. By the end of summer 1964, a loss of £400,000 was recorded. The reason for this was stated as being due to the level of sales being 20% to 25% lower than anticipated. It was felt that the policy at this time should be directed towards break-even in 1965, although it was felt that this would not be fully achieved until 1966. Contributory factors for the failure to achieve planned sales were said to be:

■ The new company undertook too big a task in trying to operate over 1,500 vehicles;

■ In general it was felt that the number of vans per depot had been too high;

■ There had been a general recession in the mobiling industry;

■ The rate of drivers' 'fiddle' on soft ice cream had reached higher proportions than ever before.

The valuation of the mobiling fleet on 1 January 1965 was £1,400,000 (approximately £15 million in today's figures). This was felt to be far too high and was a direct consequence of a valuation method laid down in the heads of agreement between the two parent companies.

In January 1964, Wall's mobiling and Charles Forte's Mr.Whippy joined forces to form Wall's-Whippy Ltd. This was a partnership of equals that would continue until Wall's fully acquired the company in 1966. Some Wall's depots were excluded from the amalgamation, as were some of the older Wall's vans. Seen here are two of Wall's Trojan fleet outside a Wall's depot in the early 1960s. Vans such as these were not included in the new joint venture. *Unilever*

Below right: In the troubled days after the formation of Wall's-Whippy Ltd, it helped to keep a good sense of humour. *Peter Hopkins*

Below: The Mr.Whippy journal *The Daily Sale* evolved into *Chimes*, the house journal of Wall's-Whippy Ltd. This subsequently lost its identity when it was incorporated into the *Wall's Journal*, where it rubbed shoulders with sausages and pies.

Clem's Cartoon

Parking Meters — Just what we wanted !

This tended to give an unrealistically high valuation to older vehicles and it remained a problem that would not be resolved until Wall's gained full control the following year. As previously stated, it soon became clear that Wall's-Whippy needed to reduce the number of company depots as well as the number of vehicles per depot to no more than 24 vans. Wall's-Whippy Ltd continued as a joint venture company for two years whilst struggling to get back into the black.

In 1966 negotiations between Wall's and Forte were concluded with Wall's purchasing Forte's interest and, therefore, acquiring a 100% share of Wall's-Whippy Ltd. However, Forte decided to retain its controlling interest in Mr.Whippy Australia. Although

The Mr.Whippy management tried very hard to get the large Coventry-based D. Di Mascio to join the Mr.Whippy franchise scheme. The answer was always a 'no' and Mister D. Di's was then established to compete with Mr.Whippy on more even terms.

the Mr.Whippy saga left a bitter taste in Forte's mouth, the Forte Group's involvement with the Australian arm of Mr.Whippy must have proved more fruitful. It eventually sold Mr.Whippy Pty Ltd in December 1993.

Now fully under Wall's control, the Mr.Whippy brand began a new era. An era where company-owned depots continued to decline in a gradual move towards a fully franchised network of depots running both Wall's and Whippy vans. By 1968, the whole Wall's-Whippy operation had become fully franchised and Wall's began to see positive results from its investment and restructuring programme. Anecdotal evidence suggests that, in the better years that followed, the nationwide network of franchised dealers rose to around one hundred whilst the combined fleet numbers fell to around a thousand vehicles.

At one end of the scale were the small depots running four to five vans, whilst larger depots were operating a mixed (Wall's and Whippy) fleet of up to 30 vans. Franchise agents continued to join the Wall's-Whippy family with 150 new Morrison Electrofreeze CAs being purchased in 1968 alone. During this year, the 'Good Humor' mobile ice cream parlours were introduced on a trial basis, with nationwide coverage planned as Wall's moved into the 1970s. However, this attempt to compete with the Lyons shop based Napoli brand did not prove to be a great success and was subsequently dropped from the Wall's-Whippy line-up. Dominic Facchino stayed at Wall's-Whippy for a short while, but his entrepreneurial spirit led him to pursue other business ventures.

Peter Hopkins also felt it was time for a change and, therefore, decided to leave Wall's-Whippy. He subsequently joined Morrisons (Electrofreeze) Ltd in Southampton, where he stayed for many years. Much of the Mr.Whippy story could not have been written without Peter's extremely fine memory and the documentation and pictures he made available. Morrisons' vehicle building division continued to supply Wall's-Whippy with vans until its acquisition by Robin Hood Engineering in the mid-1980s.

An interesting footnote to the Mr.Whippy story is what happened to all those early Commer/Karrier vans when they were deemed to be uneconomical to keep on the road. In 1969 the imposition of a new and costly HGV test was also to be another nail in coffin of these large vans. A widely propagated rumour at the time proffered the idea that Wall's rounded up all the Commers, loaded them onto a ship and then jettisoned them far out to sea. Nothing could be further from the truth, but in the ice cream trade, rumours abound as they do anywhere else.

However, there is a story to be told, and one that was relayed by the now late Jim Smith, who used to work in Wall's fleet maintenance. Jim now takes up the story: 'In the late 1960s, a decision was made to start withdrawing from service some of the Commers in the Mr.Whippy fleet. A decision was made to sell the vans at auction in Birmingham after the Mr.Whippy branding was removed and just leaving the pink and cream paint. This turned out not to be the best of ideas, as many of the vans came back into use as counterfeit Mr.Whippy vans using names (in our type-style) such as Mr.Woppy or Mr.Whirry; the lesson was learnt and no more vans were sold.

'An enterprising dealer from South Wales called "Jones" then negotiated a deal that would necessitate the vehicles being broken-up and the saleable parts exported. The vans were taken to a scrapyard at Sharpness Docks near Gloucester, which is probably where the "dumped at sea" rumour originated.

'The engines and generators were exported by container to Hong Kong, where it's believed that the engines went into junks and the TVO generators went over the border into China to generate an electrical power supply on communal farms. With other useable parts, such as the Carpigiani machine, removed the vans were then scrapped.'

This programme of scrapping the Wall's-Whippy Commer fleet has meant that the MTS- and Electrofreeze-built vans have become rarer than hens' teeth, with only a few known examples still working today. By comparison, the Mister Softee fleet declined slowly in numbers over the years and, as a consequence, just a few more have survived the ravages of time.

Unfortunately, a detailed history of Mr.Whippy after Wall's fully acquired the brand in 1966 remains a mystery. Despite many years of research, post-1966 archive material stubbornly refuses to surface, despite the enthusiastic help of the Birds Eye Wall's archives at Unilever. A detailed account of how the Mr.Whippy brand progressed after the acquisition by Wall's will, unfortunately, not be told here. Of particular interest here is *Chimes*, the house journal of Wall's-Whippy Ltd, later to become simply the *Wall's Journal*. Any reader with copies of this journal is urged to make contact.

The Brand Image

COMPANIES spend a lot of time and money developing their own distinct brand image. Sometimes a brand is so successful that its name enters public consciousness to become a generic term for a whole group of products. In the case of soft ice cream, it would be quite unusual to hear someone say 'do you fancy a Rossi, a Wall's or a Nestlé?' The term Mr.Whippy has simply become a by-word for a soft ice cream served directly to the customer from a machine. It's now simply part of the language. If Wall's ever decided to bring back the Mr.Whippy brand, this generic factor would have to considered carefully.

Back in 1959 the Mr.Whippy product range was almost non-existent compared to today's wide range of wrapped lines. Vanilla ice cream, ice-lollies and family packs were all that was on offer, but the public nevertheless lapped it up. By the 1960 summer season a fuller range of products became available, including Sundaes, Boats, and Dairy Flake cones, all backed up by full colour point-of-sale material for the vans' windows.

From the very start, Mr.Whippy realised the need for strong, forceful publicity to establish brand recognition. When a new area was opened up, large advertising space in the local press was taken out to announce the arrival of Mr.Whippy. Company publicity at the time — 1962 — stated that establishing the brand was being achieved by 'the heavy use of national television coverage'. This is certainly debatable.

The slogan 'freshly made for you' really meant what it said when Mr.Whippy was launched back in 1959. Not only was the ice cream being made on the vans, the liquid ice cream mix was also being made fresh at the factory on a daily basis and transferred to bottles kept in the van's chiller compartment. However, as good a

Here we see three incarnations of the Mr.Whippy trademark. To the left of the traditional Mr.Whippy man is the offering from New Zealand and to the right is the image that took over from the original in Australia and can still be seen today.

After the successful pilot schemes in Birmingham and London in 1959, the Mr.Whippy brand became fully established ahead of the 1960 season. The vans were now in full livery with colourful 'point of sale' material. Adverts in the local press and some limited TV coverage helped Mr.Whippy quickly move from obscurity into national prominence. Sundaes from 1/-, cones from 6d, fruit and banana boats 2/-, and fresh whipped cream in a 'Strawberry Fare' at 1/3d. *Peter Hopkins*

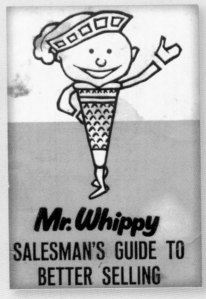

Right: Mr.Whippy was very keen to promote a universal brand image for its new company, as were its competitors Mister Softee and tonibell. To this end it produced a 10-page booklet to assist driver training. *Bob Staff*

product as this was, it was not practical in terms of shelf-life and, therefore, its distribution to an expanding fleet. When production moved to regional suppliers, ice cream mix would be supplied in polythene bags inside cardboard boxes.

This eventually gave way to sterilised liquid mix in — US gallon — cans when Wall's introduced 'Wallsiwhip'. Canned sterilised mix was a fairly new technology developed by Lyons in the mid-1950s, but one that was not without initial problems. It wasn't just a simple case of putting fresh mix into a sealed can. The ultra high temperatures used in this process could (and did) adversely affect the taste. However, with taste difficulties soon resolved, the 'tin can' became *de rigueur* until tetra pack technology was introduced.

The first Mr.Whippy mix was formulated by L. J. Hynds at Meddocream in conjunction with Dominic Facchino. Tudor Dairies of Henley-in-Arden produced the fresh pasteurised mix for the Midlands and Mylo's of Chiswick did the same for the London area. As Mr.Whippy expanded, mix production went to York-Jones of Droitwich, Northern Dairies of Hull and the Perfect Flavour Ice Cream Co of London; the last-named was soon to come under the growing Mr.Whippy umbrella. In 1959 the customer choice was severely limited, with only vanilla cones at 3d and 6d, family packs and ice-lollies making up the range. However, this limited choice did not stop salesmen regularly achieving the sort of takings that today's mobilers can only dream of.

By the 1960 season, when franchise operations got fully underway, the now familiar Mr.Whippy brand became fully formed. Sundaes and Banana Boats were introduced, with toppings from Margetts of Dalston, London. Ice cream cones at this time were supplied by Askeys of London, as Facchino Biscuits had ceased manufacturing ice cream cones and wafers.

In these early years, Mr.Whippy concentrated on the ice cream products that were freshly made on the vans, with wrapped products taking the back seat. Sundaes from one shilling (5p), Banana Boats two shillings, vanilla cones were now from 6d (2½p) with Dairy Flake and Sundae Cones costing 9d. A triple dairy treat called 'Strawberry Fayre' was also available at 1s 3d. Some Mr.Whippy operators were rather sceptical about the policy of promoting the more expensive lines 'as an adult confection in its own right'. However, by all accounts, the sales figures showed that the more expensive lines did indeed exceed expectations.

In the very early 1960s, the sight of one of these pink and cream giants would have made quite an impact, on both children of the time and on established mobilers. 'Children's loyalties on my round crumbled when Mr.Whippy arrived,' said one retired mobiler. In Coventry for example, the 30+-strong D. Di Mascio fleet was a household name. So much so that most children referred to an ice cream as a 'D. Di'. The late Ugo Di Mascio was reported as saying 'only when Mr.Whippy came along did the Di Mascio stranglehold on children's affections get seriously damaged'. Up and down the country, as soft-ice franchised operations expanded, a similar story was told.

Over the years ice cream vans have been used to promote all sorts of wide ranging products and today that is still very much the case. Here we see Robby Staff posing for the camera in his early 1960s Mr.Whippy van, as part of a nationwide Australian milk campaign. Modern digital technology in the film studio was used to change Rob's van from Pink and Cream to Blue and White. *Robby Staff*

By the mid-1960s the image of a Mr.Whippy van was certainly synonymous with the Rootes Group and its popular forward control Commer/Karrier chassis. I would imagine that, for our older readers, it is this image that has endured over the years! This is why we chose a Commer for the front cover of our book.

Unlike the Smiths-built Mister Softee Commer, which changed little through its production run, MTS developed two variants, with Electrofreeze designing the final and some say best Commer chassised model. The original model designed and built by MTS of Feltham was on a 30cwt chassis with a rearward facing twin drip-fed machine. The second being of a similar design on the shorter 20cwt chassis, with a single — pump-fed — rearward-facing machine.

From 1962 to 1965 the same 20cwt chassis was employed with a more space efficient design and rear-mounted forward-facing machine. All these models are now extremely rare with only a handful having survived the breaker's yard. Like the shade of the paint on London's red buses and the green used by the top people's store, Harrods, Mr.Whippy was distinct in its own specific shade of pink and cream. The cream — British Standard Buttermilk — was easy to track down, but the pink was a completely different proposition. For the author having an unrestored 1961 Mr.Whippy van in preservation, this meant that tracking down the correct shade was an important factor with regard to a future restoration.

However, at some point after Wall's acquired Mr.Whippy, it opted for a lighter shade of pink, with the older vans being repainted in the new shade. Not having any luck in the UK, an Australian friend managed to track down an original Queensland paint supplier to Mr.Whippy from the 1960s, who was still in business. More importantly, the company still had the early 1960s paint codes.

Mr.Whippy Overseas

THE concept of exporting the Mr.Whippy brand was probably not lost on the management team at the Leamington Spa head office. However, in the early days, establishing a strong national brand, through a network of company-owned and franchised operations, was the obvious priority. This, coupled with the need to ensure product and vehicle supply through partnership and acquisition, gave little time to consider exporting the Mr.Whippy brand. By contrast, the UK operators of the American Mister Softee brand had, from the outset, envisaged a lucrative export market, particularly in countries where Lyons was already established.

In 1959, Mister Softee (International) Ltd was incorporated and, as a result, quickly established several overseas operations. Dominic Facchino must have watched with great interest in the knowledge that there was a big market out there ready to be developed. It must be remembered that Mr.Whippy — launched on a shoestring — did not have the advantage afforded to Mister Softee by its association with an international company of stature.

However, by summer 1962 the scene was set for Mr.Whippy to be launched into what would become the largest mobile soft ice cream franchise outside of the United States and the UK at that time.

Mr. Whippy Australia

After unusually brief but fruitful negotiations with Australian businessman, Bill Kendell, the first batch of 10 Whippy vans left Southampton on the MV *Himalaya* bound for Sydney, Australia in September 1962. After many weeks at sea, the ship berthed on 22 October in Sydney harbour, from where the vans were driven through Sydney to the first Mr.Whippy depot at Rockdale.

John Hiscott, formerly depot manager Southampton and the new Sales Supervisor for Mr.Whippy Pty Ltd, recalls: 'There were some very uneasy moments for us, such as when it was thought that the doorways to the depot were not high enough to allow the vehicles through; and this only three days before their arrival. Also the time when it seemed that the drivers employed to operate the vans would have to take another test because the vehicles weighed more than two tons. This was not so bad, at least not until we were told that there was a four-week waiting list for driving tests in this category.'

A lot of problems had to be overcome, whilst engineer Sam Kingham, from Electrofreeze, worked round the clock, to get four vans on their rounds within four days and the following six vans a few days later.

In a promotion by Revlon Cosmetics, Mr.Whippy vans line-up outside Myers Department Store in Melbourne's city centre. Each van carried a pretty Revlon girl. *Bob Staff*

Taken in Australia *circa* 1965, Don Swaffer (left) and Bill Kendell pose for the camera. *Peter Hopkins*

In 1962, Sam Kingham from Electrofreeze and John Hiscott depot manager, Southampton, second and third from left, join their new Australian colleagues Pat McCabe, Jack McMurtie and John Garnham. *Peter Hopkins*

The response by the Sydney public to 'new style' soft ice cream was, to say the least, enthusiastic, but Australia's largest city is spread over a very wide area and the Rockdale depot obviously could not cover the whole area, so in January 1963, a substantial new depot at Silverwater in the west of the city was opened to receive the bulk of the second batch of 24 vans. Within a few years, Mr.Whippy would expand into every state and, in 1966, was listed on the Australian Stock Exchange, with the Forte Group maintaining the controlling interest. However, the dream was not to last, and, in just a few short years, the Mr.Whippy fleet started to decline. In many areas there were continual problems with local authorities, and in some cases these councils were quite vociferous in their stance towards mobilers. This, along with parental concerns over safety and the enormous opposition from the business community, made life for some very difficult indeed. But this was just part of the story; the cost of maintaining these large vehicles to a high standard was said to be far too expensive, and the impact of supermarkets and the rapid growth in home freezer ownership were just further nails in the coffin.

The company, therefore, decided to cease operating a mobile fleet in favour of Mr.Whippy static sites. In 1968 the first Mr.Whippy Ice Cream parlour was opened and the last of the vans was said to have been sold off by 1970. However, anecdotal evidence indicates that this was actually completed at a later date. Bill Kendell at this time decided to resign and sell his interests in the company. In 1987 the company was delisted from the Stock Exchange and became a wholly-owned subsidiary of the Forte Group. In December 1993, after just over 30 years involvement with the Mr.Whippy brand, Forte sold out to Bonlac Foods Ltd. When

Here is a survivor, which is still working in Queensland today. Back in the early to mid-1960s, importing these vans from the UK was a very costly affair due to transportation costs and the high Australian import taxes. Owner Robby Staff is seen here serving from the van he lovingly restored a few years ago. *Robby Staff*

the first edition of this book was published In 2003, Mr.Whippy Pty Ltd was owned by South African born businessman, Stan Gordon from Melbourne. Today Mr.Whippy Australia is still owned by Stan but is now part of the Franchised Food Company and branded through a chain of static sites.

MR.WHIPPY NEW ZEALAND

Early in June 1964 a decision was made to break into the New Zealand market on a totally franchised basis with one or more agents. General Foods Ltd, the dominant ice cream supplier in New Zealand at the time, agreed to take on the Mr.Whippy franchise with an expected 24 vans to be shipped ready for its 1964 summer season. Again the public's acceptance of Mr.Whippy in New Zealand was enthusiastic, and van numbers grew close to an estimated 50 vehicles at its peak. The Kiwi version of

The running Mr.Whippy man trademark is clearly seen here on this Isuzu van. New Zealand is the only country still to run officially a fleet of Mr.Whippy vans, albeit in orange and white livery.

Mr.Whippy is fast approaching its 50th birthday and boasts that it is New Zealand's 'most renowned soft serve ice-cream retailer' as well as a Kiwi 'National Icon'.

Although the brand has not enjoyed continuity of ownership over the years, it has, however, survived and now remains the only official Mr.Whippy brand being marketed via a mobile fleet today. Formerly owned by NZMP Ltd, the domestic arm of the giant dairy company Fonterra Co-operative Group, the current owners are Mr.Whippy New Zealand Ltd. It claims that 'Mr.Whippy is one of New Zealand's oldest and most renowned franchise systems with brand awareness reaching 97% amongst all New Zealanders'.

The 1989 owners, Taylor Freeze, restructured Mr.Whippy as a formal franchised system based on exclusive territories. In 2003, when this book was first published, the level of mobiles on the road was less than at its peak, with 36 vans operating through the same number of franchises. Mr.Whippy's new owners then embarked on an expansion plan, to continue putting more new Mr.Whippy mobiles on the road. Today New Zealand continues to be unique in operating vans under the official Mr.Whippy brand.

Mr. Whippy Spain

In the early 1960s, a Mr.Whippy operation was started on the Spanish holiday island of Mallorca. Based in Palma, the operation was in partnership with Marisa of Barcelona, the company being called Mr.Whippy (Espana) Ltd. So on 6 June 1963 (the 19th anniversary of D-Day), the first consignment of vans in shiny new Spanish livery left the Electrofreeze factory in Southampton bound for Mallorca.

'Try the New Ice Cream' became 'Pruebe el Nuevo Helado' and 'Freshly made for you' became 'Recien Hecho Para Ud!'. The convoy of Mr.Whippy vans travelled

Mr.Whippy never made it to North Africa although this picture may suggest otherwise. The photo was taken on a beach in Mallorca after a Mr.Whippy operation was set up on the Spanish holiday island in 1963. 'Try The New Ice Cream' became 'Pruebe el Nuevo Helado'. *Peter Hopkins*

The introduction of Mr.Whippy to Mallorca was, by all accounts, well received. The introduction of a right-hand-side sliding window in 1962 enabled the driver to serve customers on Spanish pavements. *Peter Hopkins*

overland via Dunkirk to Barcelona and then on to Palma de Mallorca by ferry. The French and Spanish public hadn't seen anything like a Mr.Whippy van before and, therefore, the vans attracted a great deal of attention wherever they went.

After a few days of cleaning, checks and driver-training, Mr.Whippy was ready to undergo a trial run out on the rounds. The 'Nuevo' ice cream was dispensed free on this occasion and, as can be imagined, went down very well indeed. The ice cream mix was made to the Mr.Whippy formula by the Marisa Ice Cream factory under the watchful eye of Mr Arturo Pelosi, who was also running the Mr.Whippy factory at Basildon. Meanwhile, a civic reception by the Mayor of Palma was arranged to welcome officially Mr.Whippy to the island. This event was held after a convoy of polished vans paraded through the centre of Palma. In attendance were the British Consul and the Chief of Police, along with Mr J. Morrell (Mr.Whippy Espana) and Mr Pelosi (Mr.Whippy UK). After the reception, the Mayor, Chief of Police and dignitaries inspected the vans and tried the exciting new ice cream with many exclamations of 'Muy bien'.

Van number 3 is busy serving customers in front of the Playa D'or Mallorca. Introduced in 1963, it's not known how long the brand lasted or if any of the vans have survived. These vans were identical to the UK versions except for the slogans being in Spanish. *Peter Hopkins*

53

Although a rather poor image, this Northern Ireland picture is worthy of inclusion here, due to its rarity. Note the twin sinks which clearly indicate that some early Mr.Whippy vans were fitted with both hot and cold water tanks. *Noel McCullough*

For whatever reason, Mr.Whippy did not develop any new export markets after this hectic but brief two-year period. This does seem rather strange, as both Forte and Wall's had a strong international dimension to their operations. Nevertheless, despite failing to match the Mister Softee export success, Mr.Whippy exported upwards of 200 vehicles to Australia, New Zealand and Spain. In doing so, developed their operation into a brand leader in both Australia and New Zealand.

MR.WHIPPY IRELAND

Closer to home, Mr.Whippy travelled across the Irish Sea to Dublin. Little has been uncovered about this operation, which was started in June 1963. This operation was in partnership with a Mr Brendan Bradley of Lucan Dairies. The company operated under Mr.Whippy (Ireland) Ltd and ran 12 vans. If any readers can throw more light on the operation of Mr.Whippy vehicles in Ireland, I would appreciate you making contact.

MR.WHIPPY USA

Mr.Whippy was never exported to the United States, officially that is! However, the Mr.Whippy man with his Tudor bonnet and dancing feet appears to have become the registered logo for Mister Whippy of Chincoteague Island in the state of Virginia. The story goes that a man named Lee Savage and his wife Wilma opened an ice cream shop in the 1950s called 'Dari Dream' but later changed the name to Mister Whippy and adopted the official Mr.Whippy logo.

In the early 1970s they imported about a dozen Morrison-built ice cream vans from the UK, which ran under the Mr.Whippy brand name in the yellow and white livery that was then employed in this country. In the late 1980s Mr Savage retired, closed the business and all but three of the vans were sold off. In summer 1991, the Conklin family of Chincoteague reopened the business, which is understood to

On warm summer days Mister Whippy himself makes an appearance outside this American ice cream parlour on Chincoteague Island in Virginia. Mind you, I think our Mister Whippy man seen here has put on a few pounds and where are those 'dancing' feet?
Richard Conklin

Below: In 2001, British-style coach-building returned to Chincoteague Island in the form of a new Whitby-Cummins van, or should I say truck. Note the spelling of Mister Whippy. On the door is our old friend with the 'dancing feet'. *Richard Conklin*

have been previously operating under a different name. The Conklins decided to rename the ice cream business Mister Whippy in order to match the name on the remaining vans. The business grew considerably and, in 1997, Mister Whippy moved to its present location on Maddox Boulevard in Chincoteague and, in 2001, a new van was purchased to continue with mobile sales.

The Pied Piper

To the detriment of many a mother's purse, the ice cream man's chime has often had the same effect on children as did the tune played by the Pied Piper of Hamelin. It is, therefore, no mistake that the name of the chimes used on Mr.Whippy vans was the Harvin Pied Piper. Mister Softee and tonibell had decided to commission their own distinctive tune, as Wall's had also done with its 'Stop Me And Buy One' tune earlier in the 1950s. Dominic Facchino decided to use that most English of tunes, *Greensleeves*, allegedly written by Henry VIII. Dominic must have been quite inspired by our King Henry, as the smiling face of the Mr.Whippy man also wears a Tudor style bonnet. However, it is understood that the main reason was due to the fact that the *Greensleeves* tune was royalty free.

Ron Peters of tonibell is the man accredited with the idea of replacing the mobiler's hand bell with an amplified musical chime. In 1954 he approached Harvin with a large American chime unit that employed tuned metal bars struck by hammers. He asked them if the company could produce a smaller, cheaper and more reliable unit, which it did.

Harvin took a Swiss musical box movement and attached a magnetic pick-up, which fed the sound to a speaker horn via a valve type amplifier. Although the resulting sound was good, this arrangement was rather heavy and, like the power hungry, valve-operated car radios of the period, tended to drain the battery. By the time Mr.Whippy and Mister Softee were launched in spring 1959, the transistor was a reality and had already been utilised by Harvin to produce the now ubiquitous Pied Piper chime.

Although technology has moved on with electronic chimes, many mobilers still favour the mechanical Pied Piper unit, which, it must be said, has given sterling service over many decades and, to Harvin's credit, with little need for change. In the 1960s the sound of *Greensleeves* would certainly have meant that Mr.Whippy was in your neighbourhood. This would have equally applied to tonibell, Wall's and Mister Softee with their unique and distinctive chimes. However, as these famous brands, except Wall's, faded away, their chimes began to be adopted by many independent mobilers up and down the country. Today, and for those old enough to remember, these chimes are a regular reminder of those famous brands and the golden era of mobiling, now sadly, long gone.

Above: No mention of Mr.Whippy would be complete without reference to the chimes the vans carried. The sheet music here is *Greensleeves*, which was Mr.Whippy's 'call-sign' from its launch in 1959 and is still used today as a registered trade mark by Mr.Whippy New Zealand.

Right: Dominic Facchino gave the Mr.Whippy man a Henry VIII style bonnet and 'dancing feet'. It's, therefore, no coincidence that Mr.Whippy danced to the Tudor tune, *Greensleeves. Jean Yates*

Below: The Harvin Chime equipment; the source of the familiar Mr.Whippy theme.

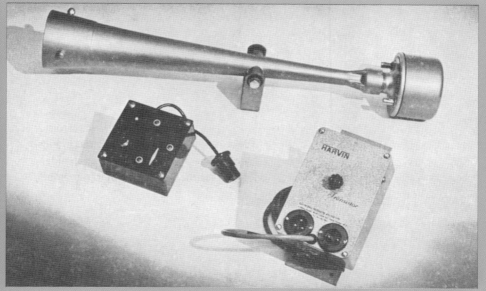

The Opposition

A T the beginning of 1959, when plans to launch both Mr.Whippy and Mister Softee were coming to fruition, the number of national ice cream brands could be counted on one hand. These were notably Wall's, Lyons Maid, Eldorado and Neilsons, all of whom ran hard ice cream mobile fleets. These brands, like independent mobilers, were all affected when they came head-to-head with the 'New Style' ice cream from the men in their large American inspired 'factories on wheels'. But who was Mr.Whippy's true opposition? Very early in the 1960s, it would be true to say that on a national level, only Mister Softee was comparable and, therefore, Mr.Whippy's only true competition. In reality this was far from the case, as the battle was different from area to area and region to region.

Although hard ice cream sales were seriously affected in those areas where Mr.Whippy depots were established, everyone still made a good living, and quality local brands continued to have a strong following. In fact it's a good time to point out that mobile sales of freshly made soft ice cream were in fact available long before the advent of Mr.Whippy, as the only thing that was really 'new' was the idea of making it on the van rather than a few hours earlier, the latter being normally the case with the small manufacturer.

Old mobilers will often argue about who first introduced 'Soft Ice Cream' to our streets, but it was in fact Mister Softee by about a month. Yet, market penetration didn't happen overnight and some areas did not see either brand for a few years, by which time other operators were getting in on the soft ice cream act.

In densely populated south London, where I worked in the 1960s, the competition was strong, with Whippy, Softee, tonibell and a host of independents such as myself vying for trade. On many occasions over those years several vans would be at the same stop, park or show together. The interesting thing was that the soft vans did not always have it all their own way; for instance, Criterion Ices of Sydenham produced a superb award winning ice cream and the public loved it. On many occasions I witnessed a longer queue at the Criterion van than at the Softee or Whippy van. When I bought my own soft van, I soon learnt to steer clear of Criterion's times on my Peckham round.

The public lapped up the idea that 'Freshly Made Just For You' produced a better ice cream, compared to a product made just a few hours earlier. Long before mobile soft-serve ice cream machines were invented, drivers such as myself would take freshly made soft ice cream — straight from open vertical batch freezers — out onto our rounds. We scooped or spooned the ice cream, which, due to the lack of high

Right: Mister Softee was officially launched to the public just ahead of Mr.Whippy in early spring 1959 when franchise holders took delivery of the first prototype vans. This was after trialling Smith's new Softee vans (and the new ice cream mix developed by Lyons) around the streets of north-west London during winter 1958.

Below left: In 1961 Mr.Whippy's factory manager, Mr A. E .Pelosi, was also the MD of the newly-launched Mr. Tasty ice cream brand based in Plaistow, east London. The vans were built by Bonallack & Sons Ltd of Basildon in Essex and were, in nearly all respects, the same as the MTS and Electrofreeze models. *Ice Cream Alliance*

Bottom right: tonibell as a brand predates the launch of both Mister Softee and Mr.Whippy in the UK. However, it was not until these two companies had proved the public's demand for soft ice cream, that tonibell converted its fleet to soft-serve vans.

overrun, had a pleasing consistency different from most of today's 'fluffy' ice creams. Ice cream made in this old fashioned way plays no part in today's commercial production of ice cream, but is, to my mind, still the connoisseur's choice.

Mr.Whippy and Mister Softee had a fairly easy time of it for a season or two after their 1959 launch, but the regional fleets and individual mobilers were soon busy converting vans to soft ice cream or buying new from the various companies offering soft-serve vans. Now competing on more even terms, the local brands would now fare much better and, in many cases, would out sell the big boys.

In Coventry for instance, the local brand of D. Di Mascio was dominant, and soon established a soft-serve fleet. So dominant were this local brand, that Mr.Whippy made many attempts, without success, to entice them into the Mr.Whippy franchise. There were, of course, some organisations, such as Curli Top and Mr. Tasty, that planned to develop fully into a national brand and, therefore, compete head-on with Mr.Whippy. This was, however, not to be.

The Wall's Ice Cream Story

As Wall's have been outright owners of the Mr.Whippy brand in the UK since 1966, it is appropriate to take a brief look at this most famous of brand names. Wall's can trace its origins back to the late 18th century, when a young Richard Wall was an apprentice in what is now part of London's fashionable West End working in a meat and pie business at St James's market. We have to assume that he was industrious as well as being ambitious, as he took over the business in 1806. As the years passed and the family business grew, Wall's products were regularly noted for their taste and quality. By the time Richard's son, Thomas, took over, Wall's were delivering its pies and sausages far and wide, including to the Royal household.

The summer months were problematic for all producers of meat products, as sales fell away as a result of the general lack of refrigeration at this time. In 1913 the business was run by Richard Wall's grandson Thomas II. It was during this period that the idea of producing ice cream was said to have originated. Legend has it that it was a young Wall's clerk suggestion that the company start to manufacture ice cream as a way to bolster sales during the summer downturn. This may or may not be true, but the actual date of birth of Wall's Ice Cream is still somewhat shrouded in mystery.

Historical dates are often problematic, with the birth of Wall's Ice Cream certainly being debatable. In a Wall's in-house journal of 1957, it states: 'When the new ice cream factory was started in Acton in 1920, it was capable of making several thousand gallons of ice cream a week.' However, in the Unilever history *Licks Sticks and Bricks*, the date is clearly put in 1922. The book states that: 'The First World War delayed his plans, but in 1922 an ice cream department was set up in the sausage factory at Acton, West London. A small vertical freezer was installed.....'

Little detailed historical evidence of this period seems to have survived, but what was about to happen next was set to change the company and introduce to the public a concept that developed into a British institution. Again, according to a 1957 Wall's in-house journal, the then Walls Managing Director, Lionel Rodd, observed a man selling boot laces from a box on a tricycle and attracting customers by ringing a hand bell. It's said that the impact on Rodd was such that he quickly built a tri-cycle with an insulated box carrier, which was understood to have cost £6. He took the tricycle out onto the streets and undertook three weeks of trials, presumably in the Acton area. The success was such that 10 trikes were ordered ready for the next summer season, which, we presume, was 1923 if you accept the date of birth published in *Licks Sticks and Bricks*.

It's not known if the author of the 1957 article in the Wall's house journal had access to documentary evidence from the early 1920s or whether he was just

repeating what had become common folk-lore within the company. However, it's understood that prior to the early 1920s, Wall's had already used a 'cool box' on a trike to deliver is meat products during the problematic summer months. The ambient temperature was reduced by the use of dri-ice. At this point the most famous slogan in mobiling history was coined *'Stop Me And Buy One'* and soon appeared on the growing number of trikes pedalled by the 'Wallsie' salesmen. Later on Wall's distributed cards with a printed 'W' that were displayed in the house window whenever the 'Wallsie' man was required to call.

Using trikes to deliver right to the customer's door was an innovation that proved a great success. In 1924 the salesmen, were issued with uniforms, boots and caps in dark blue and white, with the trikes painted dark blue. The 'Wallsie' salesman's day was arduous; he not only had to pedal up to 20 miles in his 12-hour shift, he also worked a seven-day week in the season. In the winter this was reduced to a three-day week.

Confident in its success, a second ice cream department was set-up at the firm's Manchester factory, at Godley, and more distribution depots were also established. In 1927 the company started to manufacture its own solid carbon dioxide at Acton to refrigerate the trikes. This move not only reduced costs across the business, but also reduced the weight of the trikes.

Through the 1920s Wall's Ice cream continued to expand throughout the country. Wall's also developed its first advertising campaigns, aiming to familiarise consumers with its ice cream and brand name. By this date the business was part of the Unilever organisation. In 1930 Thomas Wall died; he was the last of the family dynasty.

In 1933, Wall's started wafer production at the Friary in Acton but, by 1950, it had moved to its own wafer facility in Southall. By 1939 there were nearly 160 depots or sub-depots nationwide. Ice cream production came to a halt with the onset of World War 2 and most of the 8,500 trikes were sold off with many being utilised for the war effort. But that's another story! Post-war efforts went into mobiling from vehicles, but in 1952 the trikes returned albeit on a much reduced scale. In the late 1940s Wall's coined the phrase *'more than a treat — a food!'* This was a period of intense advertising and expansion, with Wall's Ice Cream developing into the nation's top brand in terms of visibility and market penetration.

It's not quite clear exactly when the first motorised Wall's Ice Cream vans were introduced, but the company did use Model T Fords in the 1920s to supply the growing number of mobiles and static sites. The post-war use of mechanised mobiles saw some important progress, with the 1950s producing some magical sales figures. The overall UK sales of ice cream in 1939 was £6 million and by 1950 was £14 million; by the end of the decade this figure had trebled!

As the pale blue and cream Wall's vans became a regular sight on British housing estates throughout the 1950s, the 'Stop Me and Buy One' slogan was now set to music by dance-band leader Peter Yorke, who composed the now famous five-note chime for 'Wallsie' mobiles.

As Mr.Whippy was gearing up for its 1959 launch, Wall's demonstrated its commitment to ice cream production by opening what was said to be 'the largest state of the art ice cream factory in the world'. This new factory at Gloucester is still very much in use today and remains at the centre of Wall's Ice Cream production. In 1981 Wall's and Birds Eye merged to form Birds Eye Wall's. The combined business remains a subsidiary of Unilever.

PLEASE PLACE THIS CARD IN YOUR WINDOW IF YOU DESIRE OUR SALESMAN TO CALL

Today, ice cream mobiling is totally dominated by independent operators. However, Wall's and Nestlé have both continued to promote their brands through the tried and tested franchise route. This has enabled both companies to keep their brands highly visible to the public through distinct brand imaging up and down the country.

Index

Allen, Mike 20
Askeys Biscuits 46
Austin/Morris LD..........................17, 36
Aztec Oils...15

Bedford CA/CF 20, 22, 23, 36, 39, 42
Binns, L. A. 10
Birds Eye Wall's 63
Bonnalacks 18
Bradley, Brendan 54
Buchan, Stan 16,18, 21, 23, 24
Birmingham.....6, 8, 9, 10, 12, 13, 43, 45
Bonlac Foods Ltd 50

Cake Cone Company 31
Cafe Royal......................................28, 32
Carpigiani 12, 13, 14, 16, 19, 21,
                                        25, 37, 43
Carverhill, Peter 11
Commer/Karrier........15, 17, 18, 19, 21,
                        22, 26, 29, 35, 43, 47
Commercial Motor Show........11, 12, 14
Cooper, George 13
Conklin, Richard 54, 55
Conway Brothers..................................10
Coventry Victor 7, 16
Cummins S. C. 22
Cummins Whitby 55
Criterion Ices..58
Curli Top 59

Dancing Feet 12, 55, 57
Dari Dream ....54.
D. Di Mascio 42, 46, 59
Di Mascio, Leo and John 13
Di Mascio, Ugo 46

Eldorado 9, 58

Facchino, Anthony..............6, 8, 9, 2, 31
Facchino Biscuits 7, 8, 9, 46
Facchino, Dominic 8, 9, 10, 12,
                        13, 14, 16, 18, 24, 26,
                        28, 31, 32, 46, 48
Facchino, Enrico 6, 7, 8, 9
Facchino, Joseph 9, 12
Facchino, Mary......................................6
Facchino, Paul..................................8, 9
Facchino, Philomena...........................10
Facchino, Stella 10, 12
Fonterra Cooperative Group...............52
Ford Consul 16, 19
Ford Transit 23
Forte 32, 33, 34, 35, 37, 41, 42, 50
Forte, Charles 28, 29, 30, 32, 34, 41
Frozen Assets 11, 26

General Foods 51
Good Humour 40, 42
Goodwin, Geoff....................................24
Gordon, Stan 51
Greensleeves....................12, 35, 56, 57

Harvin Chimes......................................56

Henry VIII................................12, 56, 57
Hiscot, John 48, 50
Hopkins, Peter 6, 7, 8, 10, 11, 12,
                13, 14, 19, 20, 24, 25, 26,
                28, 29, 32, 35, 37, 40, 41,
                42, 45, 49, 50, 52, 53
Hynds, L. J...46

Ice Cream Alliance..............7, 14, 17, 30,
                                33, 34, 39

Kendell, Bill 29, 48, 49
Kingham, Sam 48, 50
Kinlock, J...35
Knowles, J..35

Leamington Spa 10, 13, 48
Licks Sticks & Bricks............................60
London 10, 11, 12, 14, 26, 45
Longleys & Hoffman.............................10
Lloyd, Michael and Peter 34
Lucan Dairies 54
Lyons.................9, 13, 40, 46, 48, 58, 59

Margetts of Dalston 46
Maynard, Ted 24
McCabe, Pat 50
McCullough, Noel 54
McMurtie, Jack 50
Marisa of Barcelona......................52, 53
Meddocream. 8, 9, 13, 46
Mister Softee 10, 12, 13, 14, 16,
                17, 18, 19, 23, 34, 43, 45,
                48, 54, 56, 58, 59
Morrell, J. 53
Morrison (Electrofreeze)
Southampton 13, 16, 18, 19,
                20, 21, 22, 23, 24, 26, 29, 39,
                42, 43, 47, 48, 50, 52, 54
MTS of Feltham............7, 11, 12, 16, 17,
                18, 19, 24, 43, 47
Mylos Ice Cream ...10, 11, 14, 16, 18, 46

Nestlé 44
Newman, Terry.....................................23
Northern Dairies ...14, 17, 26, 28, 29, 46
NZMP Ltd..52

Onan Generator 22, 39

Pacitto, Anthony............................12, 31
Pacitto, Ernest 10, 12, 13, 14, 16, 18
Pelosi, A. E. 24, 28, 36, 53
Perfect Flavour Ice Cream...........14, 24,
                                        28, 46
Peters Ron 30, 56
Picador 21
Pet Shop Boys......................................27

Rains Dairies...36
Relph, Walter 8, 22
Reynolds, Ken.......................................13
Roach Trailers 20, 23
Robertson, Roy.....................................26

Robin Hood Engineering 43
Rodd, Lionel 60
Rootes Group 16, 17, 20, 47
Rossis...44

Savage, Lee and Wilma 54
Smith, Jim...43
Smiths of Gateshead........10, 18, 23, 47
Sparshatts...17
Staff, Bob and Robby........45, 47, 49, 51
Sutton, Garry.......................................27
Swaffer, Don 49
Sweden Freeze 13, 37
Swedish Royal Board...................19, 21

Tarr, Colin..21
Tartaglia...20
Mr.Tasty...59
Taylor Freeze 52
Thirlwell, Edwin....................................25
tonibell 21, 30, 34, 45, 56, 58
Treat Products 30
Trojan..41.
Tudor Dairies 46
TVO 14, 15, 16

Unilever.....15, 20, 33, 36, 41, 43, 60, 62

Velocette 22
Vaughan, Ted 12

Wall, Richard and Thomas 60, 62
Warwick House 13, 35, 48
Wall's 5, 9, 13, 30, 33, 34, 35, 36,
                38, 39, 42, 43, 44, 56,
                60, 61, 62, 63
Walls Journal 41,43
Wallsiwhipp............................34, 35, 46
Wall's-Whippy 23, 34, 35, 36, 38,
                40, 41, 42, 43
Weston, Garfield 9, 10
Whitby, Bryan..................................22, 23
Whitby, Stuart 39
Williams, Harry.....................................13
Wincanton Engineering ....22.
Walter Shenson Pictures...................35.
Mr.Whippy............5, 7, 8, 10, 11, 12, 13,
                14, 15, 16, 17, 18, 19, 21, 22, 23,
                24, 25, 26, 27, 28, 29, 30, 31, 32,
                33, 34, 35, 36, 37, 40, 41, 42, 43,
                44, 45, 46, 47, 48, 49, 50, 52, 53,
                54, 55, 56, 57, 58, 59, 63
Mr.Whippy Australia 41, 44

Yates, Jean 57
York, Jones..46.
Yorke, Peter 63